A
Handbook
of

EUROPEAN ARCHITECTURAL STYLES

Wilfried Koch

D1205891

W. Foulsham & Co Ltd

LONDON · NEW YORK · TORONTO · CAPE TOWN · SYDNEY

W. FOULSHAM & COMPANY LTD
Yeovil Road, SLOUGH, Berkshire SL1 4JH

ISBN 0-572-00804-X
© 1967 Verlagsgruppe Bertelsmann
© 1980 (English Language Edition) W. Foulsham & Co. Ltd.

ACKNOWLEDGEMENTS.
The Publishers are grateful to the following for the use of photographs:
National Monuments Record; Greater London Council; Courtauld Institute;
James Austin; Bildarchiv Foto Marburg.

Printed in Great Britain by
Lowe & Brydone Printers Ltd, Thetford, Norfolk.

You too can become an expert on architectural styles

Every style in art is made up of a specific number of equally specific architectural elements. This means that it would be possible to produce a practical guide to stylistic classification by speaking of, say, a typically Romanesque (or typically Gothic or typically Renaissance) set of component parts. To put it in a simplified form, we could say that in each period the master-builders put the individual components together to create a whole new series of works of art, each one different from the other. Because the master-builders had differing temperaments, and came from different geographical and intellectual backgrounds, and of course because of the laws of statics, some of these architectural elements would sometimes be rejected, while others would be emphasized or modified; or new elements might be invented and added to the basic structure. This explains why buildings of the same period do not all create the same overall impression.

If the spirit of the times changes and the number of elements that are changed or developed afresh (as a result of technological progress or changing tastes) becomes too large, the overall impression created by a building is transformed. For the sake of simplicity, the common practice is to refer to a new phase within a single style (for instance Early Gothic,

High Gothic and Late Gothic) or to a new style altogether (Romanesque, Gothic, Renaissance and so on).

The transition from the Carolingian style to the Romanesque provides a particularly good example of this organic development within the individual elements and within the overall style. On the other hand the transition from the Gothic to the Renaissance was a great deal more abrupt, since it represented a protest against the traditional spirit of the Gothic era. In this case the various elements that went to make up the Gothic style were deliberately rejected wholesale, and replaced by models taken from Antiquity and by newly developed features. The general impression created by Renaissance architecture is that it is a new interpretation of the antique style.

This means that if you want to find out about the basic reasons underlying stylistic change in architecture, you must also study the history of ideas. Needless to say, the changes in the individual elements do not in themselves give a complete picture of the mysterious human and historical contexts that underlie any artistic development.

The aim of this book is to present a picture of the general impression created by the different stylistic eras by illustrating and comparing buildings that are particularly typical of each style. At the same time the most important features of each building are listed, since they constantly recur in other works of art in the same style. Details that can be presented only in general terms in the tabular summaries are also included in the glossary section, where they are described and sketched individually; their most important variants are also given. These variants often have different names and therefore have to appear under a new heading. The problem is that as a result you can't find them unless you know what they're called. We have helped you by keeping them as individual entries, but whenever possible grouping them together under a well-known main heading, so that you can easily recognize them by studying the illustrations. For instance all the various ornamental forms from ARABESQUE TO WAVED ROSETTE can be found together under the main heading ORNAMENT. Similarly, anything to do with the shape of the roof, ranging from GABLED STEEPLE to 'WELSCHE HAUBE', comes under the main heading ROOF TYPES. If you look up the individual entry you'll be directed to the relevant main heading, unless the main heading is already included in the entry.

Many of the illustrations in this book combine a buildings floor plan with a perspective drawing from its interior. In these cases, the floor plan will include an arrow (⚷) to indicate the position and direction of the perspective view.

The aim of the book is to give the reader enough definite images for him or her to be able, after a while, to ascribe a work of art to the correct period by studying the overall image it creates and naming its individual features. This will also allow him to distinguish between the stylistic components of the large number of 'impure' buildings he will come across (for instance works of art that were started in the Gothic era and completed during the Renaissance).

The short guides that are on sale today in every important building always contain a large number of concepts that are too abstract for the layman. But you can look them up in our pictorial glossary and find them in the building itself by first studying the illustration. We recommend that you take this little book with you whenever you travel, keeping it in your car so that you can't forget it. In particular, make sure you use it frequently – it will help you to appreciate the beauty that surrounds you and thus enrich your travels.

Antiquity

Classical antiquity has been a model for many revivals, for many new beginnings throughout the history of western architecture. In particular, the temples of Greece and Rome were treated as a touchstone by architects in many periods. The Roman temple, as will be seen later, owes much to the Greek; and the Greek developed from earlier structures in Asia Minor and further East. The type of Greek temple that is now familiar is an oblong building with columns and a gabled roof. This form was related to a more archaic house, and in fact the Greeks treated the temple as a house in which the God lived under the guise of a cult statue, which was almost always set up in the *cella* or main chamber. There were many varieties of the temple type which depended on the importance of the cult and the means of the community which built it. The simplest is known as *in antis* (1), where the columns stand between the walls; these ends are called *antae*, while the colonnade (b) through which you enter the *cella* (a) is known as *pronaos*. If, as often happens, this arrangement is repeated at the back of the building (2), the second *pronaos* usually has a blind wall behind it without any access to the *cella*. Where the temple has a range of columns running along its whole width, it is known as *prostyle* (3), and if these occur at both ends (4), it is called *amphiprostyle*. But most of the well-known Greek temples are surrounded on both long and short sides by columns, and this type is called *peripteral* (5). When the range of columns on the long side particularly is doubled – which occurs only in the largest of temples – they are called *dipteral* (6). There are also circular

ACROPOLIS
Ionic Capital.

temples usually surrounded by a single range of columns *monopteral* (7).

These arrangements made the columns the most important element in Greek architecture, and they were distinguished according to their general proportions and their ornaments into three orders: the squat, masculine Doric, which is associated with justice, war and divination; the more slender and voluted Ionic, associated with fertility and death; these two existed from the 8th century BC; in the 5th century, a third order, more slender and more elaborate, known as Corinthian, was added.

The columns and the beams they carried set out the proportions of the Greek buildings that are now so much admired, and the unit according to which the plans and details of the temples, as well as of the civil buildings, were devised, was the module that is always half the diameter of the column at its base.

The gables of the Greek temples, called pediments, were filled with sculptured groups, and the whole building, including the sculptures, was painted with harsh and brilliant colours, and often decorated with bronze and gilt attachments.

1. Temple: distyle in antis;
2. Distyle in antis at both ends;
3. Prostyle;
4. Amphiprostyle;
5. Peripteral; 6. Dipteral;
7. Circular temple, monopteral.

a. Naos or cella;
b. Pronaos;
c. Opisthodomos or rear chamber.

The orders in Greek architecture

(see also glossary, under CAPITAL and COLUMN)

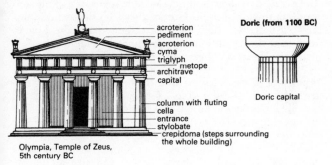

acroterion
pediment
acroterion
cyma
triglyph
metope
architrave
capital

column with fluting
cella
entrance
stylobate
crepidoma (steps surrounding the whole building)

Olympia, Temple of Zeus,
5th century BC

Doric (from 1100 BC)

Doric capital

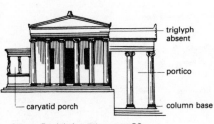

triglyph absent

portico

caryatid porch

column base

Athens, Erechtheion, 5th century BC

**Ionic
(from 6th century BC)**

Ionic capital

**Corinthian
(from 5th century BC)**

Corinthian capital

The Corinthian order retained most of the features of the Ionic (base, absence of triglyphs etc.), but substituted a new capital. This capital appeared in secular buildings some time before it was used in temple construction.

Athens, choragic monument of Lysicrates, 4th century BC

Roman Architecture

The Romans took over the Greek temple form, but also Etruscan traditions, and developed systems of arching and vaulting unknown to the Greeks; they later devised complex and vast domes. Like its Greek counterpart, the Roman temple was accessible to the priesthood, while the lay-folk performed their sacrifices and worshipped on external altars. The Romans also developed a number of new building types: the *thermae* (or baths); the *circus*; the *aqueduct*; the *triumphal arch*; and the *basilica* (or royal hall).

The Christian church, which from the outset sheltered its congregation, could not be based on the pagan temple, but took over the Roman market and judgement hall (basilica); the late Roman temple is shown here on its usual high podium, with a deep portico; and instead of the detached Greek colonnade, an ornamental one of attached columns called *pseudo-peripteral*.

The Roman temple and Early Christian church

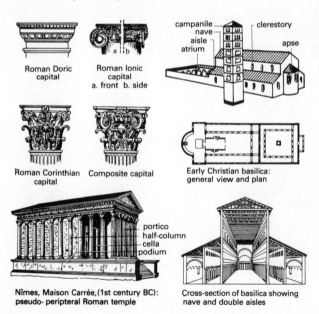

Roman Doric capital

Roman Ionic capital
a. front b. side

Roman Corinthian capital

Composite capital

campanile
nave
aisle
atrium
clerestory
apse

Early Christian basilica: general view and plan

portico
half-column
cella
podium

Nîmes, Maison Carrée, (1st century BC): pseudo- peripteral Roman temple

Cross-section of basilica showing nave and double aisles

FULDA, ST MICHAEL.

Carolingian

The period between the fall of the Western Roman empire in the 5th century AD and the coronation of Charlemagne (AD 800) is usually known as the Dark Ages, and as its name implies was marked by a great reduction of building activity.

Charlemagne initiated a policy of imperial authority in Europe, of expansion and of building, deliberately basing himself on late antique and Byzantine models, sometimes even bringing actual building materials (the columns of the Palace chapel, now part of the cathedral at Aachen) from Rome and Ravenna. The setting-up of a new imperial authority in Northern Europe initiated a period of dual and conflicting authority: that of the Emperor and that of the Pope. This dual authority is made visible in a marked growth of the western end of the Carolingian basilicas, usually known as westwork, from which the great towered fronts of the Gothic cathedrals (Durham, Lincoln, Amiens, Paris) derived.

Charlemagne himself never had a permanent residence, and several monasteries grew to provide hospitality not only for the imperial courts, but also for officials for the imperial chanceries. The cosmopolitan court of Charlemagne (his chancellor was the English monk, Alcuin of York) marked the development of European art for several centuries to come, although the empire he set up did not survive his death. It had a powerful revival under the Ottonian (Germanic) emperors, whose reign corresponded to the Romanesque period in European architecture.

Although Carolingian artistic patronage has left many relics (illuminated manuscripts, ivory and goldsmith work), there are no significant remains of Imperial dwellings or of the towns of the period, as against its churches.

St Michael (Hildesheim) is one of the most important surviving buildings from the period and shows the radical adaptations of classical building form: the massive walling and small windows; the clearly defined crossings, which establish the proportions of the whole plan, the two apses at either end complemented by the vast towers over each crossing. Note the crypt under the eastern choir, which provides a raised chancel. In such crypts appear the first vaults, which were to become an essential element in Romanesque church building.

The Roman arch is used here as both a structural and a symbolic element. The side walls are articulated by an arched colonnade on the Roman model, and the nave is closed at either end by vast semicircles, which are intended to recall the form of the Roman triumphal arch. The form of the blocked capital with its impost, which is used at Hildesheim, as it is later throughout Western Europe, is a further simplification of Byzantine examples and represents the final reduction of the classical orders.

Carolingian architecture, 8th century — AD 911

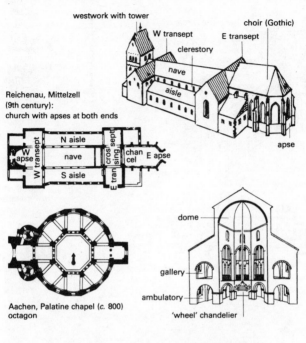

westwork with tower

W transept

E transept

choir (Gothic)

clerestory

nave

aisle

apse

Reichenau, Mittelzell
(9th century):
church with apses at both ends

W apse

W transept

N aisle

nave

S aisle

E transept

crossing

septe

chancel

E apse

Aachen, Palatine chapel (*c.* 800)
octagon

dome

gallery

ambulatory

'wheel' chandelier

flat wooden ceiling

clerestory

triumphal arch

wall-paintings

frieze

round-headed arcade

entrance to crypt

columns
with capitals

Reicherau, Oberzell (9th century): interior, looking east

Ottonian architecture: AD 911—1000 (1030)

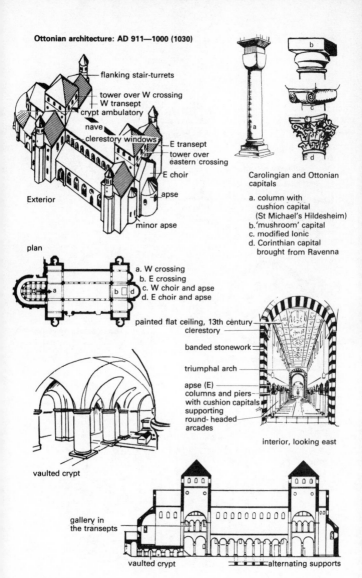

- flanking stair-turrets
- tower over W crossing
- W transept
- crypt ambulatory
- nave
- clerestory windows
- E transept
- tower over eastern crossing
- E choir
- apse
- minor apse

Exterior

plan

a. W crossing
b. E crossing
c. W choir and apse
d. E choir and apse

Carolingian and Ottonian capitals

a. column with cushion capital (St Michael's Hildesheim)
b. 'mushroom' capital
c. modified Ionic
d. Corinthian capital brought from Ravenna

painted flat ceiling, 13th century clerestory

banded stonework

triumphal arch

apse (E) columns and piers with cushion capitals supporting round-headed arcades

interior, looking east

vaulted crypt

gallery in the transepts

vaulted crypt

alternating supports

St Michael's, Hildesheim, early 11th century, with double choirs. longitudinal cross-section

14

SERRABONNE
Romanesque Arcaded Gallery.

Romanesque Architecture

As the great movements of the Celtic and German peoples in the North and of the Arabs in the South were finally halted by the Atlantic coast, as well as by the headlong crash on the Pyrenees, Europe's new population was reorganized in a settled pattern with the Emperor at the top, and a descending hierarchy of temporal lords, each one of whom held land from his immediate superior. This order was echoed by an ecclesiastical order headed by the Pope;

15

the two orders were closely intertwined, and are known as the feudal system. On the lowest rung were the farmworker and the small craftsman, who exchanged their labour and accepted a limitation on their freedom in return for protection. Fortifications were therefore a dominant form of the period. Walls were thrown up round towns; castles became important centres for the defence of the surrounding district, as well as landmarks; even some of the more important churches were fortified, and when that was not necessary, they were still given symbolic battlements and towers.

The bearers of lay literacy were the troubadours and the minnesingers. But the dominant cultural centres were the monasteries, and later the cathedral schools, which provided not only the clergy but also the civil service of Europe. As counsellors and teachers of the temporal lords, and kings, their influence was often much greater than their actual power. They were frequently artists, as well as patrons of the arts. Musical life was dominated by the Gregorian chant, and pious donors increasingly bequeathed land to the religious foundations which themselves became great temporal lords. The vast areas of wall in the churches and castles invited 'important', sculptured treatment of the surround of any opening, as well as the imagination of the story-teller and the painter. This was one of the great periods of European wall painting.

The wealth of the monasteries attracted the envy of princes, but also heart-searching among the monks. The cry for reform is one of the permanent features of European monastic life. The most important at this period was that emanating from Cluny, which was founded in 909/10 and became the centre of a world-wide organization.

As a foil against the rich and powerful Cluniac monasteries, another reform that sprang from the Abbey at Cîteaux (founded 1098) was devoted to the greatest asceticism and simplicity. Its monks built vast but undecorated churches in inaccessible places on neglected land (Fountains in Yorkshire), raising the standard of European agriculture, which the monks practised assiduously.

The rise of the new national monarchies and the developing power of city-states led to a weakening of feudal ties, to a rise in the standard of living and the greater security of the settled population, in spite of continuous warlike activity.

frieze of round arches
flanking towers
crossing tower
dwarf gallery
lesene
lucarne
apse (W)
round window
round-headed window

exterior from the west

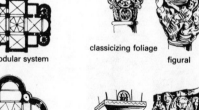

clerestory window

wall shaft

aisle window

Speyer,
original design of 1050
(vaulted in 1090)

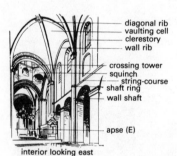

diagonal rib
vaulting cell
clerestory
wall rib
crossing tower
squinch
string-course
shaft ring
wall shaft

apse (E)

interior looking east

Capitals

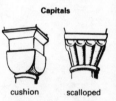

cushion   scalloped

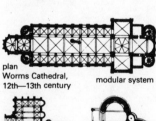

classicizing foliage

figural

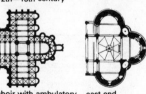

plan
Worms Cathedral,
12th—13th century   modular system

choir with ambulatory
and radiating chapels

east end
with trefoil plan

with palmette
motif   with animals

17

Romanesque 1000—1200 (1250)

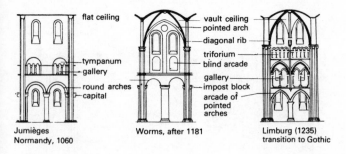

flat ceiling

tympanum
gallery
round arches
capital

Jumièges
Normandy, 1060

vault ceiling
pointed arch
diagonal rib
triforium
blind arcade
gallery
impost block
arcade of pointed arches

Worms, after 1181

Limburg (1235)
transition to Gothic

Vaults

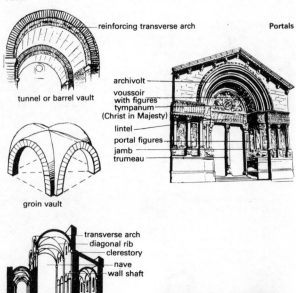

reinforcing transverse arch

tunnel or barrel vault

groin vault

Portals

archivolt
voussoir with figures
tympanum (Christ in Majesty)
lintel
portal figures
jamb
trumeau

transverse arch
diagonal rib
clerestory
nave
wall shaft
aisle

vaulting system in nave and aisles

Arles, St Trophîme (late 12th century): plan. A high point in the development of the late Romanesque portal

Romanesque — special building types

Churches of the Reform Orders (Cluniac and Cistercian)

Developmental differences
return to a flat ceiling no gallery
string-course (often with
billet moulding)

cushion capital with
semicircular patterns

arcaded basilica
(usually) no crypt

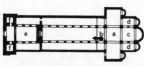

Paulinzella, ruins, 12th century
(Hirsau school)

a. *chorus major* (for choristers)
b. *chorus minor*
   (for non-choristers)
c. chancel
d. choir aisles
e. open narthex or atrium
   at the west end
f. west towers

Fortified churches

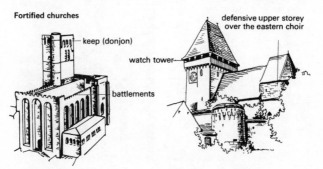

keep (donjon)

watch tower

battlements

defensive upper storey
over the eastern choir

Agde, S. France, 9th century
and after. Romanesque.

Eibesdorf, Siebenbürgen,
completed in the 15th century.
Gothic.

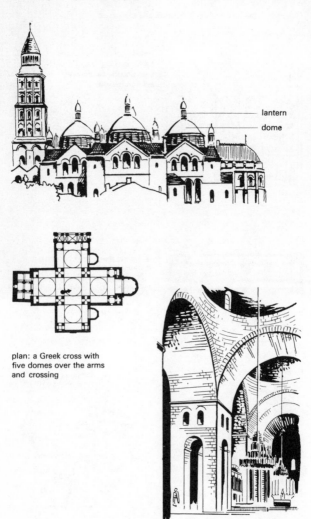

lantern
dome

plan: a Greek cross with
five domes over the arms
and crossing

Pèrigueux, S. front, begun *c.* 1120. Byzantine influence, probably derived from Italy
(St Mark's in Venice). Centrally planned.

CHARTRES CATHEDRAL
Gothic Flying Buttresses.

Gothic Architecture

In the thirteenth century the great monastic and cathedral schools of France were alive with ideas. The invention of the skeletal Gothic structure, its walls blazing with brightly coloured glass and its vault borne within the church by rows of columns, and on the outside by a poised hierarchy of buttresses, has been credited to a single man, Suger, the Abbot of Saint Denis, outside Paris (1081-1151). The vault took on the ribbed form characteristic of Gothic architecture, and the arches became pointed, allowing greater freedom in manipulating the arcaded bay in relation to it. The liberating of the vault from its supporting wall prompted the Gothic masons' drive to build ever higher, which culminated in the choirs of the 13th-century French cathedrals, particularly Beauvais (1225), whose vast spire collapsed in 1573.

The style quickly spread from France throughout Europe, assuming particular features in different countries. French masons reduced the westwork to twin-towers, separated by a wall usually pierced by a rose-window, a feature that in its turn had come from Italy. In Germany the towers were crowned by great open-work spires; in the North and East a sparely moulded and very linear brick architecture developed. In Spain the great volumes of the church were emphasized by the distance between the choir and the altar. In England the ribs of the vault became an almost independent patterning device, which in the 15th century gave rise to the fan vault.

The rise in population figures and the privileged position of certain townsmen led to the growth of old and the founding of new towns. While the monasteries were concerned with land and agriculture, the cathedrals grew up in the old settlements and were involved with the organization of the city, which depended on the banding-together of the different trades and crafts into semi-religious societies (guilds), whose headquarters, usually halls, became the model of all civic building. These came to be built in stone and assumed proportions that rivalled those of palaces and castles.

The new urban population, however, was outside the guilds and the old urban organization. It was for these, and for the roving rural workers, that the new begging (mendicant) orders were founded by St Francis of Assisi and St Dominic. Like the older orders, they soon attracted men of learning (Albertus Magnus, Thomas Aquinas to the Dominicans; Bonaventura to the Franciscans) and became great builders. But while the older churches were dedicated to the liturgy, the newer orders were almost equally concerned with preaching, and preferred the hall church to the older basilica.

The medieval castle was sometimes engulfed by the city, but many remained isolated. Their outlying defence, particularly on low ground, was a moat filled with water, within which stood a battlemented wall. The entrance was usually protected by a flanking tower (barbican), the curtain wall was pierced by a fortified gate and access was over a drawbridge. The keep or donjon were both a look-out and the final stronghold of the castle's besieged defenders. Westward of the Rhine, they also usually contained the living quarters. The chapel was often an important part of the castle and farm-buildings were frequently enclosed within the curtain wall.

Elements of Gothic architecture   **Vaults**

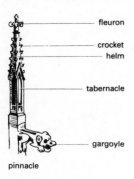

fleuron
crocket
helm
tabernacle
gargoyle

pinnacle

quadripartite and sexpartite
rib vaults

net vault   stellar vault

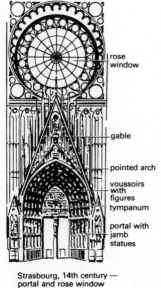

rose window
gable
pointed arch
voussoirs with figures
tympanum
portal with jamb statues

Strasbourg, 14th century —
portal and rose window

Capitals

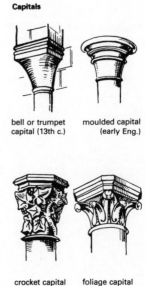

bell or trumpet
capital (13th c.)

moulded capital
(early Eng.)

crocket capital   foliage capital

Elements of Gothic architecture
Tracery windows

trefoil

quatrefoil   mouchette

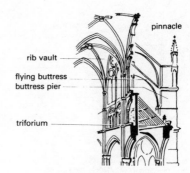

pinnacle

rib vault

flying buttress
buttress pier

triforium

section showing triforium and
buttressing system for vaults

Tracery forms:
a. and b. *circa* 1200
c. and d. 13th – 14th century
e. and f. 15th century

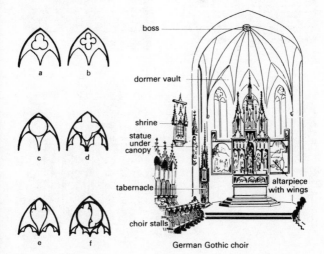

a

b

c

d

e

f

boss

dormer vault

shrine

statue
under
canopy

tabernacle

choir stalls

altarpiece
with wings

German Gothic choir

25

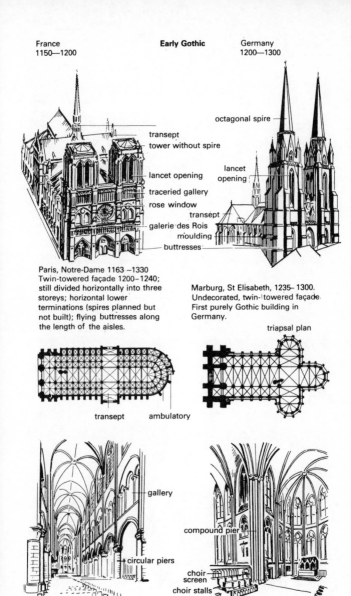

France
1150—1200

Early Gothic

Germany
1200—1300

octagonal spire

transept
tower without spire

lancet opening

traceried gallery

rose window

transept

galerie des Rois

moulding

buttresses

lancet opening

Paris, Notre-Dame 1163 –1330
Twin-towered façade 1200–1240;
still divided horizontally into three
storeys; horizontal lower
terminations (spires planned but
not built); flying buttresses along
the length of the aisles.

Marburg, St Elisabeth, 1235– 1300.
Undecorated, twin-ltowered façade
First purely Gothic building in
Germany.

triapsal plan

transept   ambulatory

gallery

circular piers

compound pier

choir screen

choir stalls

26

Early Gothic

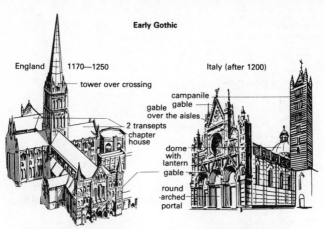

England   1170—1250

tower over crossing

Italy (after 1200)

campanile gable

gable
over the aisles

2 transepts

chapter house

dome
with
lantern

gable

round
arched
portal

Salisbury, cathedral, 1220—58
No west towers, but a very large
tower over the crossing. Much
surface ornament on the west
front. Only a few flying buttresses.

Siena, cathedral, 1229—1350.
Built of marble. Campanile to
one side, not integrated into the
body of the church.

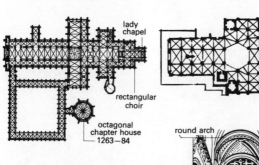

lady
chapel

rectangular
choir

octagonal
chapter house
1263—84

round arch

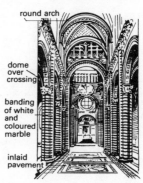

dome
over
crossing

banding
of white
and
coloured
marble

inlaid
pavement

The transition from one style to
another (e.g. Romanesque to
Gothic) is always gradual. It varies
from region to region, and within
each region from building to building. Certain features characteristic
of a particular country may be
said to produce a national style;
but not all monuments in that
country will necessarily show
those features.

High Gothic

France 1200—1275 (1300)

Germany 1260—1400

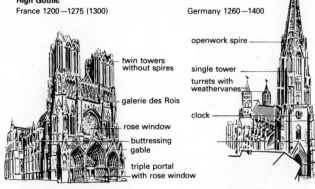

twin towers
without spires

galerie des Rois

rose window

buttressing
gable

triple portal
with rose window

openwork spire

single tower

turrets with
weathervanes

clock

Rheims, cathedral (1211—1311).
Twin-towered façade c. 1295,
rich in sculpture and ornament.
(Portals with statuary and stained
glass, gables, finials, crockets,
fleurons, rose windows, etc.)

Freiburg, minster (1190—1513).
Single-towered façade with
spire. Later examples are
completely suffused with tracery
which breaks up the division of
the storeys. (Ulm, Vienna).

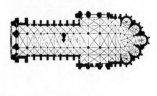

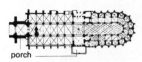

porch

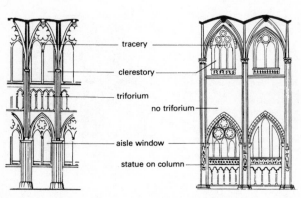

tracery

clerestory

triforium

no triforium

aisle window

statue on column

28

England 1250 – 1350

Spain from 1200

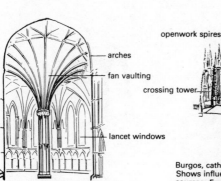

openwork spires

arches

fan vaulting

crossing tower

lancet windows

Lincoln, chapterhouse, second half of 13th century. An example of English Gothic fan vaulting.

Burgos, cathedral (1221 – 1567). Shows influence from various sources: French twin-towered façade and rose window; Moorish elements in the Plateresque style of the crossing tower; Renaissance balustrades.

plan of chapterhouse

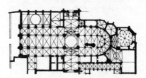

below: Wells, cathedral, c. 1139. The strainer arches of the crossing tower.

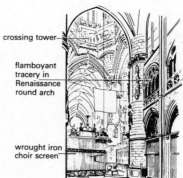

crossing tower

flamboyant tracery in Renaissance round arch

wrought iron choir screen

Late Gothic, 14th — early 16th century

Summary of the development towards late Gothic ecclesiastical
architectural forms. Most examples are late Gothic.

Basilica

Nave with clerestory windows
and separate roof; two or more
aisles; often transepts. The brick
Gothic of the North German
coastal area shows little or no
French influence. Decorative
elements are largely omitted in
favour of patterned brickwork
and the use of strong plain
architectural shapes.

Hall Church

Found especially in Germany.
Aisles and nave of equal height,
under a single roof. The intricate
web of ribs of the late Gothic
reticulated and stellar vaults
appears on the plan; these vaults
are particularly developed in the
hall churches of Upper Saxony.

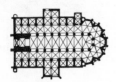

Wismar, St Nikolai, 1380—1460

Annaberg, St Anne, 1499—1520

Late Gothic, 14th — early 16th century

Summary of the development towards late Gothic ecclesiastical architectural forms. Most examples are late Gothic.

Aisleless church

Nave without aisles and usually without transepts. Common in Italy. Reached a peak in England with the large Tudor chapels at Cambridge (King's College), Windsor (St George's) and Westminster Abbey in London (Henry VII's Chapel). All three have rectilinear Perpendicular tracery and fan vaulting, in which the many small ribs serve no structural purpose.

Centrally planned building

Correspondingly even development on all sides around a pivotal central area. See pages 15 and 22. Very rare in Gothic architecture. The tower-like central focus of the Liebfrauenkirche in Trier stands on the square of the crossing.

London, Westminster Abbey, Henry VII's Chapel, 1500—1512

Trier, Liebfrauenkirche, after 1242

MANTUA ST ANDREA.

Renaissance Architecture

The firm hierarchical tissue of medieval society was softened and dissolved by the growing cities, particularly those of Italy and of Northern Europe (the Hanseatic League). The papacy, weakened by pressure from its protectors, as well as by that from its enemies, lost some of its commanding authority. A nostalgia for the greatness of antiquity, known from Greek and Latin writers and from the ruins of ancient buildings, seemed to possess the whole of literate Europe. In 15th-century Florence the movement became visible in a number of extraordinary buildings, which incorporated features both from antiquity and from Early Christian art and architecture, the work of Filippo Brunelleschi.

Renaissance means rebirth: as the Florentines invoked the virtues and power of Republican Rome, so Christian princes all over Europe saw themselves as types of the virtuous and pious rulers of antiquity: of Augustus or Marcus Aurelius, or best of all, the first Christian Emperor, Constantine.

The papacy returned to Rome early in the century, and as its power over its ancient city grew, so the rulers of the Church tried to restore some of its former glory to what was the greatest of all the pilgrimage centres: Rome itself. Its apogee was reached at the beginning of the 16th-century in the reign of Leo x and Julius II when Leonardo, Michelangelo, Bramante and Raphael were all working for the Papacy. St Peter's (p. 38) employed the last three of these artists, and was first designed by Bramante as a centrally planned, cruciform church; the arms of the cross covered by coffered barrel-vaults, and the crossing roofed by a huge dome, modelled on the antique one of the Roman Pantheon.

Although it was later modified, this Greek-cross plan with its dominating dome, as well as other centralized, domed forms (square, circle, as in 1 & 2) became the ideal church type. Custom, however, was attached to the basilican plan; and in reconciling the ideal with custom, the Renaissance devised the barrel-vaulted basilica with a domed and apsed space at the altar end, sometimes even using a succession of domical compartments (3 & 5). There was, however, no ancient precedent for a façade of a church with a high nave and low aisles, and the usual solution of this element was arrived at by the marrying of the triumphal arch with the temple front, as well as the contrivance of reconciling the lower and upper storey by means of giant volutes (4).

The church façade relied on ranges of columns for its plastic effect: the ancient orders were the chief, inevitable ornaments of architecture. Their revival was furthered by the new invention of printing, which allowed the rapid spread of old and new treatises (Vitruvius, Alberti), as well as of pattern-books (Serlio, books on the orders). The aims of such authors were not always fully appreciated by architects in Northern Europe, unfamiliar with the ancient

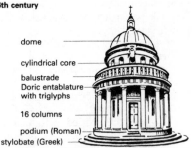

dome

cylindrical core

balustrade
Doric entablature
with triglyphs

16 columns

podium (Roman)
stylobate (Greek)

1. Rome, Tempietto at S. Pietro in Montorio; by Bramante, 1502. Based on the model of an antique circular temple

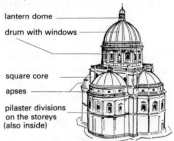

lantern dome

drum with windows

square core

apses

pilaster divisions
on the storeys
(also inside)

2. Todi, S. Maria della Consolazione, begun 1508. High Renaissance

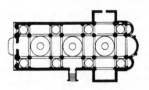

3. Venice, S. Salvatore, 16th century. Modular plan; domes over nave, crossing and aisles

examples. The pattern-books, in particular, gave rise to an architecture in which medieval practice was continued and developed, but covered with a surface, often fantastic, of classical detail.

This is particularly evident in German, Dutch and Northern French domestic architecture, in which the basic Gothic framework is divided into ornamental compartments, and scrolls, obelisks and dormers are used to produce constantly varying outlines.

The growth of internal security within the city brought

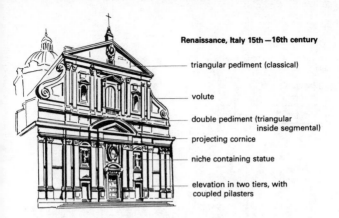

triangular pediment (classical)

volute

double pediment (triangular inside segmental)

projecting cornice

niche containing statue

elevation in two tiers, with coupled pilasters

4. Rome, Il Gesù by Vignola and Giacomo della Porta, 1568—75. The design of this late Renaissance Jesuit church in Rome, both inside and out, had a strong influence on Baroque ecclesiastical architecture (p.47). The transition between the broad ground floor and the narrower upper storey is accomplished by large volutes. Five segmental and triangular pediments, arranged above each other, emphasize the central axis.

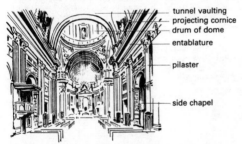

tunnel vaulting
projecting cornice
drum of dome
entablature

pilaster

side chapel

5. Rome, Il Gesu, interior: the aisles have been transformed into chapels. The church proper consists of the barrel-vaulted nave, and, linked with it, a centrally planned space containing the altar and covered by a dome. The interior was given its Baroque form in the 13th century.

about the opening of the lower storeys of large buildings and the development in Italy of the *palazzo* type: often with lettable space (shops, warehouses) towards the street, one or more colonnaded courtyards, and its main reception rooms on the first floor (*piano nobile*). While stone and stuccoed brick became standard materials in the South of Europe, timber framing continued to be used in the North.

At the same time the growth of national armies and the invention of gun-powder revolutionized the practice of warfare, rendering many of the old defences obsolete and

35

Architectural elements of the Renaissance

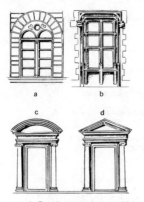

a. early Renaissance window with round
   arches and surround; Italy, 1450
b. rectangular window with mullions
   and transom; France, 1500
c,d. windows framed by columns bearing
   segmental and triangular pediments;
   Italy, early 16th century

a. grotesque capital
b. column with candelabrum decoration
c. cartouche with strapwork surround,
   especially popular in the Netherlands

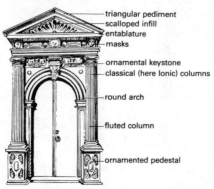

triangular pediment
scalloped infill
entablature
masks

ornamental keystone
classical (here Ionic) columns

round arch

fluted column

ornamented pedestal

German Renaissance doorway

centrally planned building (Z) with
barrel-vaulted nave added, (see text, 35)
a. central dome
b. arms of the original Greek cross
c. subsidiary domes
d. nave
e. apses

(Rome, St Peter's 1506—1667)

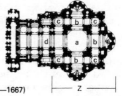

36

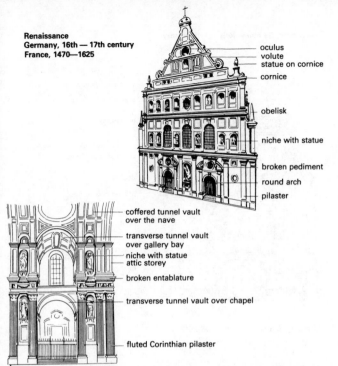

Renaissance
Germany, 16th — 17th century
France, 1470—1625

— oculus
— volute
— statue on cornice
— cornice

— obelisk

— niche with statue

— broken pediment
— round arch
— pilaster

— coffered tunnel vault over the nave

— transverse tunnel vault over gallery bay
— niche with statue
— attic storey

— broken entablature

— transverse tunnel vault over chapel

— fluted Corinthian pilaster

Munich, Jesuit church of St Michael (Hofkirche), 1583—97. façade, and elevation of one bay of the nave.

increasing the break between town and country.

Medieval church building was largely sufficient for the needs of the 16th and 17th centuries in the north of Europe. Renaissance church building is therefore fairly sparse, and has the eclectic character that has already been noted in domestic building (p. 36). Nevertheless in the 17th century the type represented by the Gesù church in Rome (4 & 5) replaces the Gothic and superficially classicizing buildings (pp. 64 & 65), though the adaptation is sometimes curiously far-fetched, as at Saint Gervais in Paris (p. 41).

The criticism of institutions led to a break in the religious unity of Europe; the demands for reform crystallized in the Lutheran and Calvinist movements. The beginning of the wars of religion marks the end of the Renaissance proper.

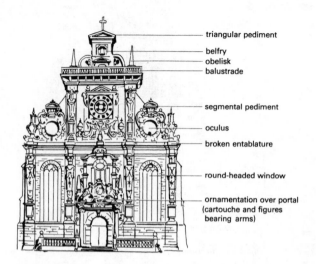

triangular pediment

belfry
obelisk
balustrade

segmental pediment

oculus

broken entablature

round-headed window

ornamentation over portal
(cartouche and figures
bearing arms)

Bückeburg, Stadtkirche, dedicated in 1615

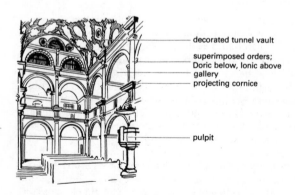

decorated tunnel vault

superimposed orders;
Doric below, Ionic above
gallery
projecting cornice

pulpit

Augustusburg, castle chapel, 1570—73

Renaissance, France, 1470—1625

Dijon, St Michel, first half of the 16th Century. Twin-towered façade of Gothic origin with Renaissance decoration and domes, built on to a Gothic church; model of a round temple above the central portal.

Paris, St Gervais, façade 1616, interior Gothic. The tall façade (whose arrangement is unrelated to the church behind), with its three tiers of coupled columns, already suggests the Baroque. It was often imitated in France and in other countries.

STEINGADEN
Baroque ceiling decoration.

Baroque Architecture

In Germany and the Low Countries, as well as in parts of France, the Reformation was almost as much a social as a religious movement. The Peasants' War was the first of a long series of religious/national campaigns of which the Thirty Years' War (1618-48) was the most extended both in time and in geography. The reformers' destruction of the statuary and the treasuries of many churches in Britain and Scandinavia, as well as in Germany and the Low Countries, was answered from the South by an emphatic manner of building and decorating, which originated in Rome at the turn of the 16th and 17th centuries. The previous period of uncertainty, often associated with the style known as Mannerism, is dominated by Michelangelo's buildings in Rome (the

Capitol, St Peter's), and Palladio's in and around Venice. Michelangelo, in particular, introduced the giant order, which became an important device of 17th-century builders.

The importance of the sermon, which has already been noted in connection with the friars' churches, was reasserted by such new, Counter-Reformation orders as the Society of Jesus (Jesuits), whose headquarters was the Gesù church in Rome, as well as by the reformers. This, and the focusing of Catholic ritual on the altar, contributed to a re-evaluation of the central plan and the atrophy of the aisles.

The plan forms, however, were no longer the squares and circles of the Renaissance, but were now based on the oval and the ellipse, and included more complex inter-penetrating shapes; this reflected the developments of cos-mology (the discovery of elliptical orbits), and the growth of descriptive geometry. But in the 17th century thinking and behaviour – and consequently architecture – were also dominated by rhetoric: persuasion seemed more important in the great age of controversy than systematic philosophy. The importance of display was emphasized by the use of new explosive materials for fireworks; set-pieces became an important, if temporary, species of architecture.

Persuasive display is therefore the dominant mood of the time. The façade becomes an almost literary confection of statues, ornamental devices and columns, like a permanent theatrical spectacle, while in the interiors illusionistic effects break or dissolve the structure, opening it, as it were, directly into Heaven.

The great development of firearms led to the devising of new systems of fortifications: the bastion and the revetment replaced the tower and the wall. Stellar and centrally developed town plans replaced the chequerboard patterns of earlier times.

Italian Baroque

From Rome the manner spread southward to mingle with Spanish emphasis and exaggeration in Naples and Sicily, and with northern earnestness in Lombardy, Piedmont and Venice. The search for effect and the demands of rhetoric were channelled through an almost obsessive con-cern with building technique and the homage to Antiquity. The interrelationship of complex plans and often apparently unrelated façades was made into a fine art. The Italian Baroque palace became a great isolated monument on which later French practice would be based.

Although French Classical architecture had matured in the 16th century, its full impact was not felt until the reign of Louis XIV, whose patronage of architecture became as important an element of policy as his wars. In centralizing not only power but cultural and social life in his vast palace at Versailles, he set an example that very many European

Baroque, Italy 1550—1800

Rome, S. Agnese in Piazza Navona; by Rainaldi and Borromini, 1652—77: façade, interior and plan. Centralized plan with four tunnel-vaulted arms; apses on the

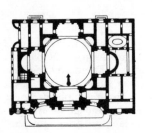

lateral arms. The square central space has niches in the corners and is covered by a dome. The façade with its twin towers, superimposed columns and pilasters, and balustrade, is focussed on the central dome.

princes would follow. In Spain a highly ornamented manner (Churrigueresque) was exported into the Spanish and Portuguese dominions of Central and South America, and adapted by local, often indigenous craftsmen into a style that sometimes seems far removed from its European antecedents.

In the decoration of the Spanish and French palaces a new manner based on grotesque and naturalistic decoration appeared, which was to have a rapid and extensive growth in early 18th-century France, under the name of Rocaille or Rococo.

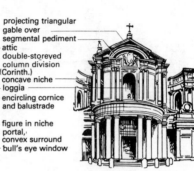

projecting triangular
gable over
segmental pediment
attic
double-storeyed
column division
(Corinth.)
concave niche
loggia
encircling cornice
and balustrade

figure in niche
portal,
convex surround
bull's eye window

Rome, S. Maria della Pace, façade;
by Pietro da Cortona, 1656—7

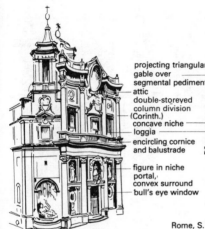

Rome, S. Carlo alle Quattro Fontane;
by Borromini, 1634—63. Façade and
plan. Undulating (concave-convex)
rhythm.

Rome, S. Andrea al Quirinale
plan; by Bernini, 1678

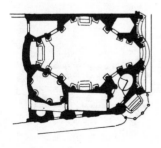

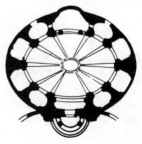

German Baroque

Large-scale building had to wait until the end of the Thirty Years' War in Germany and the defeat of the Turks at Vienna in 1683. The four plans below show the progressive emancipation of German builders from Italian precedent

Baroque,Germany, 1650—1800

Munich, St Cajetan, Theatine church; 1662—67. The first domed church in Bavaria, built on the model of Roman Jesuit churches. The architects were Italian and French.

Weingarten, abbey church, 1715—23. Tunnel vaulted church with gallery, apsed transepts and choir, and dome on a drum. The architects were Italian and German.

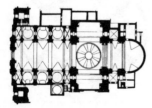

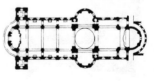

and the adaptation of the Rococo forms, of secular origin, to an ecstatic and elaborate church architecture dependent on the complexity of novel centralized planning, and often in sharp contrast to the sober but elaborately roofed and domed exteriors.

Secular architecture adopted much the same manner; its most splendid example is the Residenz at Würzburg, where the French precedent of entry through a *cour d'honneur*, and a monumental staircase, brings the visitor to a *piano nobile*. The principal rooms look away from the entry (or town) side over formal gardens, which are arranged to appear infinite.

Steingaden, Wieskirche, 1746—54. Around both the elliptical main area, with its false 'mirror' vaulting, and the elongated choir runs a narrow ambulatory of the same height, forming a twin-shell structure. Richly stuccoed.

Steinhausen, St Peter and St Paul, 1728—33. Centrally planned, with an ambulatory running round the oval nave (cf. the Wieskirche). illus. shows detail of stuccowork from capitals to painted ceiling.

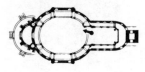

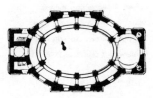

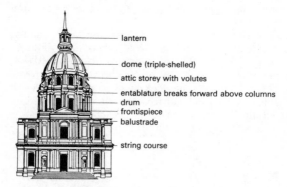

- lantern
- dome (triple-shelled)
- attic storey with volutes
- entablature breaks forward above columns
- drum
- frontispiece
- balustrade
- string course

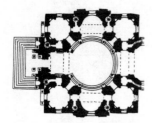

Paris, dome of Les Invalides; by Jules Hardouin-Mansart, 1675– 1706. Strict mathematical division of ground plan and elevation, based on a unit which is the radius of the central area.

Santiago de Compostela, cathedral. Highly ornamented twin-towered façade of 1738 with Baroque staircase, added to the Romanesque church of 1078—1128.

Baroque and Rococo

twisted or
barley sugar column

putto

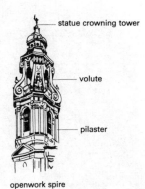

statue crowning tower

volute

pilaster

openwork spire

rocaille (rococo ornament)

statue on pediment
urn
broken entablature
cartouche set in scrollwork and
garlands
impost block
semicircular tympanum
term or herm

pilaster

column

pedestal

doorway

ST BLASIEN
Domed building in the Classical style.

Classicism

The term 'classic' is applied generally to any art that pays marked homage to Greek and Roman antiquity and is concerned with propriety and the rules of composition. In that sense, much of the architecture, as well as the painting, sculpture and literature, of 17th-century France is often more properly called classical than Baroque. In Protestant countries the Baroque style was never properly accepted. In England, although some of the buildings of Vanbrugh and Hawksmoor may be called Baroque, it is difficult to apply the term to the more sober architecture of Sir Christopher Wren, whose most famous building, St Paul's Cathedral, was to be much admired by 18th-century builders in France. From the beginning of the 18th century, moreover, England was dominated by the classicizing mannerism of Andrea Palladio.

In the narrower sense classicism, or rather neo-classicism, is applied to European art between 1760 and 1830, which was to draw its inspiration increasingly from Greek (as against Roman) antiquity. More primitive Greece, with its democratic constitutions and simpler manners, represented for the thinkers of the late 18th century an ideal that seemed much closer to their own aspiration of a return to nature and a concern with the direct expression of feeling, as against the assertive and stilted rhetoric of the earlier age.

The rising power of the middle class was absorbed into the English social structure much more easily than in France, where it led to a break with aristocratic and monarchical government in the Revolution of 1789. In Germany the social transformation was much more gradual, as was industrial growth; but it was a German working in Rome, J. J. Winckelmann, who formulated the artistic ideals of the new movement in the slogan 'noble simplicity and quiet grandeur'. Winckelmann was both an archaeologist and the first of a new breed of historians with scientific aspirations. He was fortunate enough to live at the time of the discoveries of Pompeii and Herculaneum, as well as of the first accurate publication of Greek monuments.

The Neo-classical movement had no use for the complex geometry of the Baroque. The movement returned to an almost obsessional concern with the cube, with simple rectangular planes – and with the sphere. The emphasis on this kind of geometry led to the flattening of ornament, however elaborate. The popularity of the line engraving was an ideal medium for its propagation. The beginnings of mass production allowed designers to select ornament almost as if from a catalogue. The vast growth of the archaeology industry created the need for a new kind of civic monument, the museum, formulated at the end of the 18th century, which was to become a shrine that was almost as important as the church and the town hall of earlier times.

The growth of cities at this time produced a spate of civic secular monuments that were heavily influenced by neo-classical ideas (Regent Street in London, Rue de Rivoli in Paris, Unter den Linden, Neue Wache and the Schauspielhaus in Berlin, Königsplatz in Munich, the Piazza del Popolo in Rome).

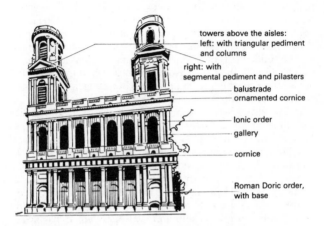

towers above the aisles:
left: with triangular pediment
and columns
right: with
segmental pediment and pilasters
balustrade
ornamented cornice

Ionic order
gallery

cornice

Roman Doric order,
with base

Paris, St Sulpice, 1646, façade 1733—77. A portico in two tiers with
horizontal emphasis. The orders are used in 'chronological' succession,
from Doric on the ground floor to Corinthian on the left tower

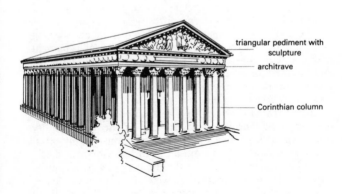

triangular pediment with
sculpture
architrave

Corinthian column

Paris, La Madeleine; by Vignon, 1806—24. Peripteral temple in
Roman Corinthian style: steps, flanked by low walls, lead up to the portico.

50

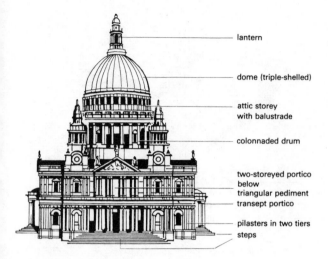

lantern

dome (triple-shelled)

attic storey
with balustrade

colonnaded drum

two-storeyed portico
below
triangular pediment
transept portico

pilasters in two tiers
steps

London, St Paul's Cathedral; by Sir Christopher Wren; 1675—1710. English
architecture remained largely outside the main currents of European
development, passing from the Renaissance to Palladian classicism with little
awareness of the Baroque.

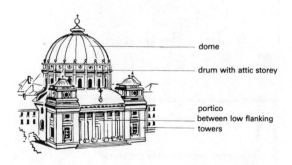

dome

drum with attic storey

portico
between low flanking
towers

St Blasien, monastery church, 1768—83. Twin-shelled dome over a circular
central space, attached to a long monastic choir. On either side are courtyards,
and palatial monastic precincts.

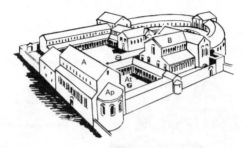

Ingelheim, 770. Reconstruction. The basilican structure on the left (A) is
the imperial hall, or *aula regia.* In the apse (Ap) stood the Emperor's throne.
The atrium (At), with its open colonnade, connected the *aula* with the
five- aisled basilican church (B). Lodgings and services lie on the far side.

Romanesque

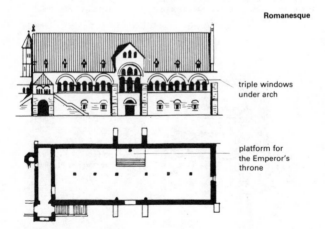

triple windows
under arch

platform for
the Emperor's
throne

Goslar, 1050—12th century, restored in the 19th century. Two superimposed
halls about 48 x 153 ft., each divided down the middle by piers.

diagram of a medieval
castle on the continent

1. keep
2. turret
3. gatehouse
4. outer gate
5. hall
6. bower
7. chapel
8. farm buildings
9. well
10. outer bailey
11. enclosing wall,
    enceinte

An English Norman castle,
Castle Hedingham (Essex), 11th — 12th century:
view and plan of the keep, and interior of the main
hall on the second storey.

53

beaver-tail roof

pavilion roof

chapel

gables

pointed windows

Marienburg, castle-monastery of the
Teutonic Knights; 13th –15th century,
much restored in the 19th century
and after the Second World War.
Heavily fortified layout with
three ranges.

winter refectory showing
tierceron vaulting.

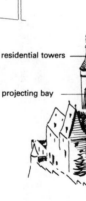

residential towers

projecting bay

Burg Eltz on the Moselle, 12th –16th century.

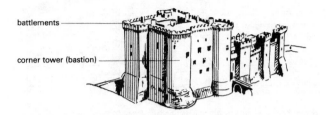

battlements

corner tower (bastion)

Tarascon, S. France, 12th – 15th century. A lower fortified wing with battlements
is joined to the block-like main castle.

1. barbican (now occupied by a
church)
2. east barbican
3. inner bailey
4. arsenal
5. outer bailey inside double
enclosing wall
6. approach

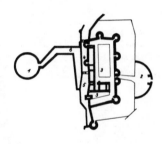

Carcassonne, S. France, 12th – 13th century, much restored in the 19th century.
Built over a Roman fortified enclosure. Castle and town, encircled by a double
ring of walls, have a completely medieval character.

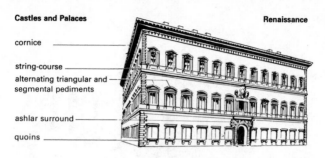

cornice

string-course

alternating triangular and
segmental pediments

ashlar surround

quoins

Rome, Palazzo Farnese by Antonio da Sangallo 1534—50. Clear, horizontal
division of the storeys with a concealed roof. Curves and straight lines contrasted
in windows and doorway.

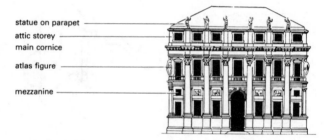

statue on parapet

attic storey
main cornice

atlas figure

mezzanine

Vincenza, Palazzo Valmarana; by Palladio, 1566. The two main storeys and
mezzanine are linked by a giant order.

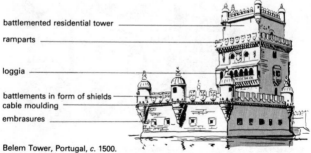

battlemented residential tower

ramparts

loggia

battlements in form of shields
cable moulding

embrasures

Belem Tower, Portugal, c. 1500.
A typical example of the Portuguese 'Gotico Oceânico', contemporary with
the Renaissance in Italy.

Heidelburg Castle, Friedrichsbau,
1601–4. Strong emphasis on the vertical
elements, in which pilasters alternate
with statues. Ornate gables with scrolls
typical of N. Europe.

Azay-le-Rideau (Loire), 1518—27.
Castle built in a lake. Battlements with
ornate gables between corner tourelles
with sharply pointed roofs.
Fortifications now largely decorative
(pseudo- embrasures), for show rather
than protection.

Aschaffenburg (Gm), castle 1605—14.
Symmetrical layout of four wings
around a quadrangular inner courtyard,
on the French model. At the corners,
four massive towers with corresponding
stair-turrets inside the courtyard.

Blois (Loire), c. 1520. Stair tower.
The ramp of the stairway is enriched
with lavish Renaissance ornamentation
to resemble balconies.

57

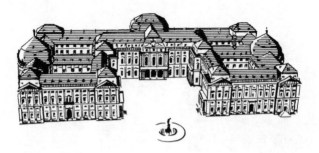

Würzburg, mansion, 1719—46. Side facing the town. Giant order connecting the ground floor and upper storey via (small) mezzanine storeys. The corners are emphasized by wing pavilions. Courtyard, garden and lateral façades have a central pavilion.

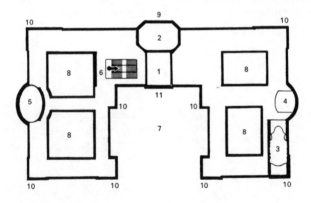

1. 'white room'
2. Imperial hall
3. church
4. dining hall
5. theatre
6. staircase

7. cour d'honneur
8. inner courtyards
9. central pavilion on the garden front
10. 8 corner pavilions
11. central façade, facing town

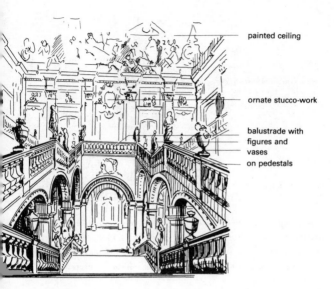

painted ceiling

ornate stucco-work

balustrade with
figures and
vases
on pedestals

Würzburg, grand staircase.

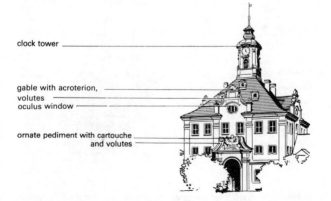

clock tower

gable with acroterion,
volutes
oculus window

ornate pediment with cartouche
and volutes

Schloss Altshausen, gatehouse, 1731—32. An unpretentious building which
nevertheless displays essential elements of the Upper Swabian Baroque.

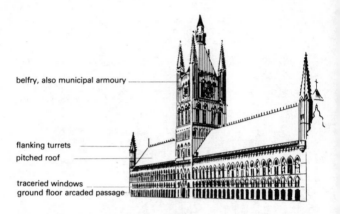

belfry, also municipal armoury

flanking turrets
pitched roof

traceried windows
ground floor arcaded passage

Ypres, Belgium, Cloth Hall, 1302—80. Destroyed by the Germans in the 1914—18 war. The three-storeyed building is about 144 yds long and is covered with tracery decoration. It testifies, as do similar imposing town halls, markets and guild halls in Flanders, to the wealth and commercial initiative of the merchants who built it.

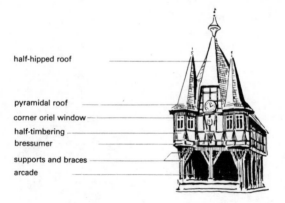

half-hipped roof

pyramidal roof
corner oriel window
half-timbering
bressumer

supports and braces
arcade

Michelstadt, town hall, 1484. Half-timbering is the preferred construction method for Gothic urban buildings. The ground floor arcading indicates the transition to the Renaissance style.

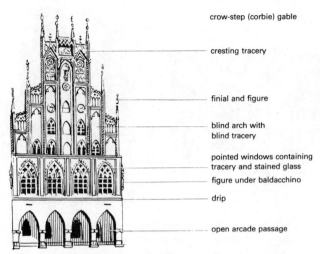

crow-step (corbie) gable

cresting tracery

finial and figure

blind arch with
blind tracery

pointed windows containing
tracery and stained glass

figure under baldacchino

drip

open arcade passage

Münster, Germany, town hall, 14th century. The liking for lavish display on the façades of town buildings is particularly marked north of the Alps. Despite the strong horizontal lines of the string-courses on the lower storeys, the vertical predominates.

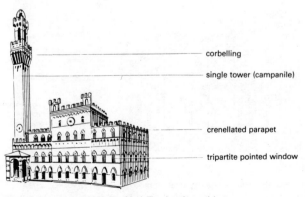

corbelling

single tower (campanile)

crenellated parapet

tripartite pointed window

Siena, Italy, town hall, 1289. The block-like elevation anticipates Renaissance palazzi. (see p. 58) (see p. 58)

(left) Florence, Palazzo Gondi, inner court, 1498. No matter how massive
the façades of Italian Renaissance palazzi might appear, their rectangular inner
courts, with arcades, balustraded stairs and fountains, impart an elegant classicism.
(right) Amsterdam, row houses, 17th century. As in Germany, the house fronts
are somewhat naive, though ingenious, adaptations of Renaissance forms
to façade designs that are still basically Gothic.

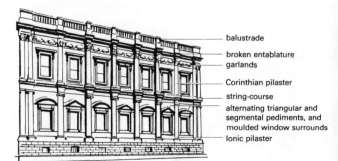

— balustrade

— broken entablature
— garlands

— Corinthian pilaster

— string-course
— alternating triangular and
segmental pediments, and
moulded window surrounds
— Ionic pilaster

London, Banqueting House, Whitehall, 1619—22. An excellent example of the
influence of Palladio on Inigo Jones. This style was revived in the mid-18th Century,
and called Palladianism.

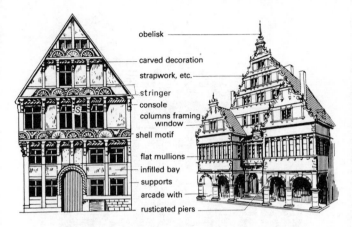

obelisk

carved decoration

strapwork, etc.

stringer

console

columns framing window

shell motif

flat mullions

infilled bay

supports

arcade with

rusticated piers

(left) Höxter, Hüttesches Haus, 16th century. (right) Paderborn, town hall, 1614—16.
These two façades illustrate almost all the important elements of decoration and
construction of the German Renaissance.

Esslingen, town hall, c. 1600. Front and rear views of Gothic half-timbered structure;
(right) a gabled stone façade with an astronomical clock and small bell-tower;
(left) a typical example of the juxtaposition of half-timbering and stone building
in the German Renaissance.

Brussels, three houses in the Grand' Place: La Rose, L'Arbre d'Or and Le Cygne,
1698—9. The restricted space within fortified towns forced vertical, as against
horizontal, expansion. Flemish Baroque builders, in particular, were inclined
to pile up, ostentatiously but chaotically, the fashionable decorative elements.
The 29 stately guild- houses in the Grand' Place, which with the Gothic town hall
and the Maison du Roi form a large square, contain all the repertoire of ornament
that one meets on the façades of Renaissance and Baroque palaces:
PEDIMENTS, WINDOW surrounds, the classical ORDERS, including the GIANT ORDER
(centre building), BALCONIES, CARTOUCHES and garlands (ORNAMENT), BALUSTRADES,
VOLUTES, OBELISKS, and statues on the cornices. In this rich ornamentation,
the prosperous bourgeoisie sought to emulate the buildings of the aristocracy.
Almost every historical style known to the builders is ransacked to provide
the details.

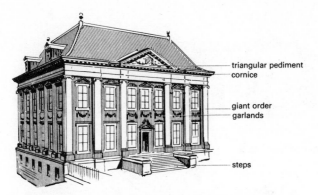

triangular pediment
cornice

giant order
garlands

steps

The Hague, Mauritshuis, 1633— 44. The façades of the Northern Baroque style
were influenced by the restrained classical austerity of Italian models (PALLADIO).
The roofs, however, are not hidden by the cornices.

Wasserburg am Inn, Kernsches Haus, 1780. Rococo. The burghers' houses of
the period display the same exuberance that characterizes the Southern Baroque
churches. Oriel windows, arcades and painting, as well as decorative stucco, give
façades a somewhat sugary domestic appearance, markedly different from the
serious ostentation of the palaces or the solemnity of the churches, from which
the decorative motifs were derived.

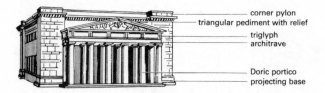

corner pylon
triangular pediment with relief
triglyph
architrave

Doric portico
projecting base

Berlin, Neue Wache; by Schinkel, 1816—18

acroterion

Munich, Glyptothek; by von Klenze, 1816—30

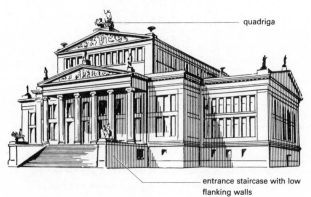

quadriga

entrance staircase with low
flanking walls

Berlin, Schauspielhaus; by Schinkel, 1818—21

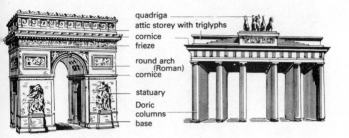

quadriga
attic storey with triglyphs
cornice
frieze
round arch
(Roman)
cornice

statuary
Doric
columns
base

Paris, Arc de Triomphe;

by Chalgrin and others, 1806—36

Berlin, Brandenburg Gate, 1788—91

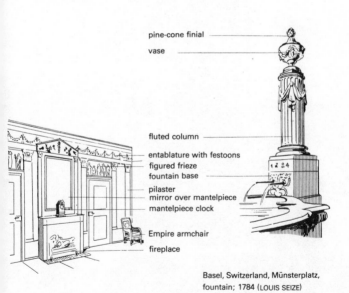

pine-cone finial

vase

fluted column

entablature with festoons
figured frieze
fountain base
pilaster
mirror over mantelpiece
mantelpiece clock

Empire armchair

fireplace

Basel, Switzerland, Münsterplatz,
fountain; 1784 (LOUIS SEIZE)

Basel, Switzerland,

Christsches Gut, c. 1810

BATH. The Great Bath, foundations date from 1st to 3rd Century; restoration and reconstruction date from 1890.

CASTLE HEDINGHAM, Essex. Norman. 11th Century
The Keep from the North West.

69

*LAYER MARNEY, Essex. Medieval. 14th Century
Layer Marney Hall from South East.*

HAMPTON COURT PALACE, Richmond upon Thames.
Tudor 1530.

*HATFIELD HOUSE, Hertfordshire. Jacobean 1611
East Wing of Courtyard.*

72

ST PAUL'S CATHEDRAL, London, Wren 1650
View from Peter's Hill.

BLENHEIM PALACE, Oxfordshire. English Baroque 1705
East front and gardens.

74

CHISWICK HOUSE, London. Palladian Revival 1725
From the South East; Burlington Lane.

BEDFORD SQUARE, London. Georgian 1750.

ST PANCRAS STATION, London. *Victorian Gothic 1868 Station and Hotel c 1880.*

Abacus
Flat slab on the top of a
CAPITAL on which the
ARCHITRAVE rests

Abutment
Solid support absorbing
the thrust of an ARCH, VAULT
or bridge.

Acanthus
Ornament based on the
luxuriant, broad, scalloped
leaf of the acanthus plant
and used on Corinthian and
Composite CAPITALS and as
a decorative motif after
400 BC. It was re-adopted
during the Renaissance and
Baroque periods.

Acroterion
Plinth for a statue or
ornament placed on the
apex and at the lower
corners of a PEDIMENT.

Aedicule
Ornamental architectural
frame, or niche, with
COLUMNS or PILASTERS at the
sides and generally with a
PEDIMENT. Originally the
setting for a sculpture in a
Roman temple.

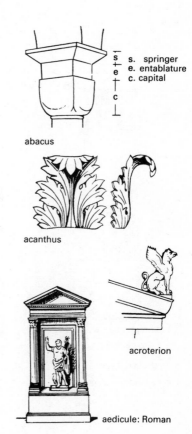

s. springer
e. entablature
c. capital

abacus

acanthus

acroterion

aedicule: Roman

79

aisle

o. clerestory
c. triforium
a. aisle

tabular altar

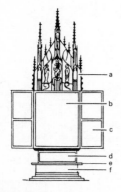

triptych altar: Gothic

a. decoration
b. shrine
c. volet
d. predella
e. mensa
f. stipes

Aisle

Space to one or both sides of a central area, or NAVE, usually divided from it by COLUMNS or PIERS. The CHOIR or TRANSEPTS of a church may also be aisled. In modern usage, a gangway.

Altar

1. Raised structure with a flat top on which sacrifices or offerings to a deity were placed in Antiquity;
2. Raised structure consecrated to the celebration of the Eucharist. After the Reformation, a 'holy table' of wood replaced the altar in England.

A Christian altar may incorporate a TABERNACLE (housing the Sacrament); an ANTEPENDIUM (altar frontal); a RETABLE (painted or sculptured back panel) sometimes enlarged to a winged altarpiece (see below), the altar panel forming the centrepiece; a CIBORIUM or BALDACCHINO (superstructure). The altare fixum is immovable; the altare portatile is designed to be taken on journeys and may be in the form of a tabular or block altar (see below), or, commonly, a folding shrine or hinged shutters. DIPTYCH and TRIPTYCH.

The principal types of altar are:
a. Tabular (a plate on supports);
b. Block (with single, often tapered, central

support and
overhanging slab);

c. Sarcophagus
(resembling a tomb
with solid sides);

d. Winged (popular in the
15th and 16th C. in
Northern Europe with
a predella sttached to
the altar top and
supporting the central
panel, or panels, and
hinged wings.

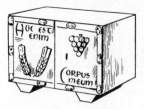

altar tabernacle—modern

Alternating Supports

Alternation of piers (P)
and columns (C) in the
name of Romanesque
BASILICAS either in a
P–C–P–C, or a P–C–C–P
pattern.

portable altar

Ambo

Elevated platform,
replaced by the PULPIT, from
which the Gospel or Epistle
were read. Traditionally the
Gospel was read from a
position to the left of the
celebrant as he faced the
altar, and the Epistle to the
right.

Ambulatory

CLOISTER or covered
walking place, generally the
AISLE extending round the
east end of a church behind
the altar.

ambo, 6th century

Amphitheatre

Oval or circular
construction surrounded by
seats in tiers. The largest
Ancient example is the
Colosseum in Rome.

Annulet

In the Doric ORDER, a
FILLET beneath the capital;
in the 12th and 13th C, a
ring round a SHAFT or shafts.

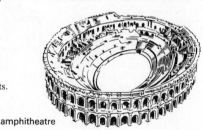

amphitheatre

antependium, Romanesque; 11th century

main and subsidiary apses

Antependium

Altar frontal of fabric or metal

Apse

Vaulted semicircular or polygonal terminal projection originating in Roman secular architecture. In early Christian churches the apse was generally at the west end, but in Byzantine and later churches it was transferred to the east end. In the Gothic period it was sometimes replaced by a square termination.

Aqueduct

Conduit, in which water flowed by gravitation to a reservoir in a town–usually an elevated structure of masonry. Roman structures survive in Italy, France (Pont du Gard), Spain (Segovia).

aqueduct

Arcade

Series of ARCHES supported by COLUMNS or PIERS. A blind, or wall, arcade is applied as decoration to a wall. A CLOISTER is a covered walk between two arcades or between an arcade and a solid wall.

a = blind arcade
b = dwarf galleries

ground floor arcade (Cologne: Church of the Holy Apostles)

Arabesque

ORNAMENT

Arch

Curved spanning structure capable of supporting the weight of superimposed masonry. It is constructed either of wedge-shaped stones, or bricks (1) or of rectangular blocks with tapering pointing. (2) The IMPOSTS (K), sometimes incorporating CAPITALS, rest on JAMBS (W) which support the first blocks, or springers (A). The intermediate blocks are the VOUSSOIRS (H) and the central one, the KEYSTONE (S). The width of the arch is the span (Sp) and the height is the rise (St). The underside of the arch is the intrados, or SOFFIT (L) and the upper surface is the extrados (R).

A stilted arch, found in Romanesque architecture has the springing-line above the imposts rather than level with them. A rampant arch has imposts at different heights.

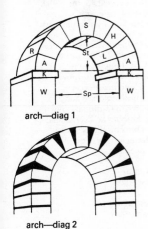

arch—diag 1

arch—diag 2

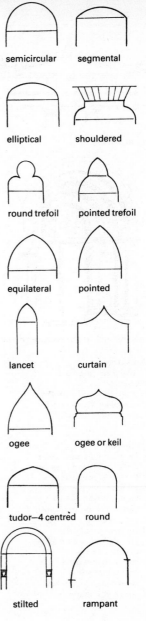

semicircular segmental

elliptical shouldered

round trefoil pointed trefoil

equilateral pointed

lancet curtain

ogee ogee or keil

tudor—4 centred round

stilted rampant

83

a = architrave

ornamental archivolt of recessed portal

Architrave

The three principal divisions of an ENTABLATURE. More widely, the moulded frame which surrounds a window or door.

Archivolt

1. Continuous semicircular ARCHITRAVE MOULDING on the face of an ARCH;
2. In Romanesque and Gothic PORTALS, each contour of the arch which continues the configuration of the portal. Archivolts may be decorated with continuous FRIEZES (particularly in Romanesque churches) or sculptural figures (in Gothic)

Arris

Sharp edge formed by the meeting of two surfaces.

Art Nouveau

Movement deeply influencing the applied arts, including architecture, which flourished briefly, but vigorously, in most European countries and the USA between 1890 and 1910. It was characterised by a sinuous naturalistic style and by the rejection of the traditional vocabulary. In Germany, the movement was known as JUGENDSTIL, and in Italy as Stile Liberty, after the London store of that name. The French sometimes refer to it as Le Style Moderne. The Belgian architects, Victor Horta and Henri van de Velde, were perhaps the principal protagonists of Art Nouveau in architecture.

Arts and Crafts Movement

Style of decorative art and architecture in England in the later years of the 19th C. in revolt against machine-made Victorian applied art. It was inspired by the work of William Morris, Norman Shaw, Philip Webb and W. R. Lethaby were prominent in the movement.

Hand made objects, natural materials and a return to traditional craft techniques and vernacular architectural types were characteristic of the movement.

Ashlar
MASONRY

Astragal
ORNAMENT

Atlas

Male figure used in place of columns or pilasters, usually to support an ENTABLATURE. Cf CARYATID

Atrium

1. In Roman domestic architecture, a central hall with an opening in the roof to allow water to be collected in a cistern below;
2. Open court in front of an Early Christian or Romanesque church.

Attic

1. Upper storey above the main ENTABLATURE of a building as in a Roman TRIUMPHAL ARCH;
2. Room situated within the roof.

Attic base

Base used with Ionic and Corinthian ORDERS consisting of two convex MOULDINGS (TORUS) with a concave moulding (SCOTIA) between.

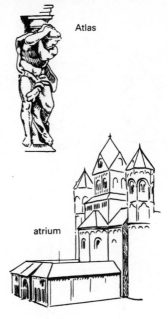

Atlas

atrium

Attic base

Attribute

Object associated with a character or figure to enhance recognition; it usually refers to a particular event in life, e. g, the trident of Neptune, the keys of St Peter

attributes–

Andrew –
St Andrew's cross

Bartholomew –
knife

James the Elder –
pilgrims dress
plus mussels

James the Younger –
standard or
walking stick

John – beardless   Judas – club   Mathew – set-square,   Paul – sword
                    (not Iscariot) axe or halbard

Peter – one   Philip – stick   Simon – saw   Thomas –
or two keys   cross   set-square or lance

Aumbry

Recess in the wall of a church to contain the sacred vessels.

balcony

Baguette

Small MOULDING of semicircular section.

Bailey

External wall of a castle or the space between the inner and the outer wall of a castle or between the inner walls and the KEEP.

Balcony

Open projection with parapet or balustrade on an upper storey, supported underneath by BRACKETS, CORBELLING, etc.

Baldacchino

Canopy, generally supported on columns, over an episcopal throne, altar or tomb. It is derived from Baldacco, the Italian word for Baghdad, and was originally applied to a rich figured silk from that place. In a more general sense, it may be used for any decorative, umbrella-like covering (e. g. for protecting the figure of a saint carried in a religious procession).

baldacchino

Baluster

Round or polygonal small column, often carved and usually swelling towards the lowest part. When supporting a rail or coping, the whole is called a balustrade and forms a parapet around flat-roofed buildings, along terraces or bridges, etc. When referring to stairs the word banister is commonly used.

Banderole

Flat, ribbon-like inscription often explaining the identity of a figure or representing his speech.

Baptistry

Place of baptism. Part of a church or a detached building, often centrally planned and circular or polygonal in form.

A substitute was a FONT placed in the body of a church.

Barbican

A defensive structure, normally a tower, to protect an entrance or drawbridge.

Barge Board

Projecting board, frequently ornamented, fixed to the eaves of a GABLE or a pitched roof to cover the rafter-ends.

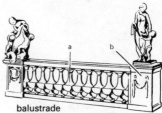

balustrade
a: banister
b: dado (portion of pedestal between base and cornice

baptistry, external and internal view.

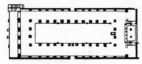

Roman basilica

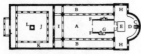

early Christian basilica

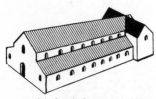

model of early Christian basilica

cross section of basilica

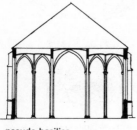

pseudo-basilica

Bartizan

Turret corbelled out from a wall.

Base

ATTIC BASE, COLUMN, ORDERS.

Basilica

1. Roman commercial exchange or hall of justice, usually aisled and terminating in a semicircular apse;
2. Early Christian church, adopted and altered in later periods. Characteristically, the NAVE (A) has a timbered roof, higher than the flanking AISLES (B), from which it is separated by colonnades. In place of the Roman TRIBUNE stands the CATHEDRA. (C), in the apse (D) behind the ALTAR (E).

   The area reserved for the altar and AMBO (G) is separated from the congregation by a CHOIR SCREEN (F). The church has TRANSEPTS (H), a NARTHEX (I), GALILEE (J), and an ATRIUM (K) with a well (L) at the centre.

Basket Grille

Iron balcony grille, especially on ground floor windows, curved in outline and often ornate in design.

Bay

Vertical internal or external division of a building, marked not necessarily by partition walls, but by units of VAULTING, ORDERS, WINDOWS, BUTTRESSES, or other distinctive repeating features.

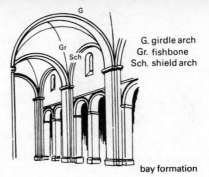

G. girdle arch
Gr. fishbone
Sch. shield arch

bay formation

basket grille

Bay Window

Fenestrated projection from the FACADE or corner of a building forming a BAY in a room. It may embrace more than one storey. A rounded bay window is known as a bow window. ORIEL WINDOW.

Bead and Reel

ORNAMENT

Belfry

1. Defensive wooden tower;
2. Bell tower or campanile. Part of, or separate from, the main building.

Bench End

Termination of a pew, often carved, sometimes topped with a FINIAL called a poppyhead.

Biedermeier Style

German and Austrian style, current *c* 1815—48, reflected in furniture, interior decoration and painting. The term comes from the names of two comic German philistines, Biedermann and Bummelmaier, created by the writer Viktor von Scheffel in his 'Fliegende Blättern' (1848).

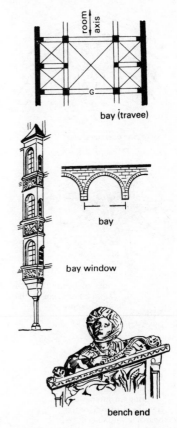

bay (travée)

bay

bay window

bench end

boss with projection to take vaulting ribs: Gothic

keystone used as boss

boss suspended between eight bosses: late Gothic, 15th century

Billet
ORNAMENT

Bishop's Throne
CATHEDRA

Boss
  Ornamental projection covering the intersection of the ribs of a vault, or the beams in timber ceilings.

Bowtell
1. Roll or convex MOULDING;
2. SHAFT in a compound PIER.

Bracket
  Projection designed for a support.

Brickwork
  Header: a brick laid with the end exposed on the wall face.
  Stretcher: a brick laid with the side exposed on the wall face.
  English bond: alternate courses of headers and stretchers.
  Flemish bond: headers and stretchers laid alternately in the same course.
  Heading bond: consisting entirely of headers.
  Gouged: brickwork very accurately laid with fine joints.

Bridal Door
  In Germany, a PORTA on the N side of some Gothic churches, before which the betrothal ceremony took place; often decorated with figures of the Wise and Foolish Virgins who await the Bridegroom (Matthew 25:1—12).

Bucranium
ORNAMENT

Bull's Eye Glass
  Early window glass, consisting of panes with a round thickening in the centre (like the bottom of a bottle) set in lead.

Buttress

Light cross-ribbed VAULTING, when it was invented, relieved the load on the walls, but increased it correspondingly at the points (normally on the pillars) where the RIBS rested. Flying (or arched) buttresses were therefore constructed to transfer the outward thrust of the vault and the weight of the roof to additional supports in the form of PIERS or buttresses outside the building. Sometimes angle, clasping or diagonal buttresses, which comprised solid masonry projections built externally against the angles of the walls, were used without the characteristic arches of flying buttresses. These made possible the extraordinary height of Gothic interiors.

early wall buttresses

buttresses

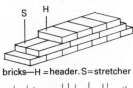
bricks—H=header. S=stretcher

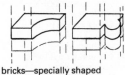
bricks—specially shaped

bull's eye pane

buttresses on choir

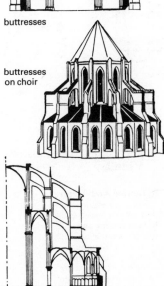
double buttressing

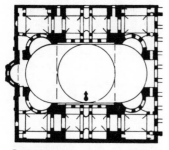

Byzantine architecture – Hagia Sophia, Constantinople

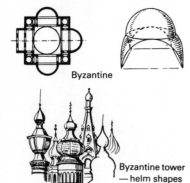

Byzantine

Byzantine tower — helm shapes

Byzantine Architecture

Christian architecture of the eastern division of the Roman Empire and its spheres of influence. It centred on Byzantium (Constantinople) and merged Early Christian, Asiatic and Alexandrian elements for the creation exclusively of religious works.

Its development falls into main epochs:

1. First flowering under the Emperor Justinian (526—565). Building of Hagia Sophia (main church of Eastern Empire in Constantinople). The Iconoclast dispute (726—843), when controversy raged over the appropriateness of the veneration of pictures or images of Christ, was finally decided in favour of the practice;

2. Second Golden Age under the Macedonian Renaissance (9th to 12th C) and its spreading influence to Venice (St Mark's) and Russia;

3. Final artistic impetus of the Palaeologian era (1263—1453. Michael Palaeologos was crowned in 1259). In 1453, the Turks captured Constantinople, since which time Byzantine art continued to exist within the Greek Orthodox Church. Its influences are traceable in German and French Romanesque and Gothic, as well as in the *maniera greca* or *bisantina* of Italian art of the 13th C.

Its distinguishing architectural form is the CENTRALLY PLANNED BUILDING with domes, which is often united with the BASILICA.

Cable Moulding
ORNAMENT

Caisson
Decorated sunk panel in a ceiling. Sometimes called a coffer or lacunar.

caisson

Campanile
BELFRY

Campo Santo
In Italy, an enclosed and usually arcaded burial ground.

Capital
Carved or moulded top of a COLUMN or PILASTER.
c.f. ORDERS.

A = abacus
E = echinus
F = flutes
G = arris

Doric column 1100 BC

V = volute;
S = shaft;
P = pulvinar;
E = egg and dart moulding

Ionic capital after 600 BC

Corinthian capital, 5th C BC
AK. acanthus
K. caulicoli

composite

scalloped capital—Romanesque

P = pipes
H = necking

mushroom capital, 9th C
K. spherical cap
Ke. spherical fluting

block capital

ornamental block capital

figured capital

late Romanesque figured capital

late Romanesque ordinary capital

palmette capital developed from block capital

transitional between Romanesque and Gothic

chalice capital

foliated capital —early Gothic

foliated capital —late Gothic

crocket capital

plate capital

Renaissance volute and acanthus capital

grotesque capital

caryatid

cathedra with 'estrade'

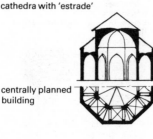

centrally planned building

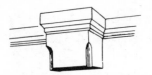

stopped chamfer

Caryatid

Female figure replacing a COLUMN or PILASTER, usually to support an ENTABLATURE. ATLAS.

Cathedra

Bishop's throne in a church. In early Christian times, situated at the centre of the APSE behind the altar. Since the Middle Ages, it is usually situated to one side of the CHOIR; sometimes splendidly decorated and with a BALDACCHINO.

Cavetto

Concave moulding, usually a quarter circle in section.

Cella

Central area of a Classical temple. NAOS.

Centrally Planned Building

Building which develops outwards and symmetrically on all sides from an architecturally emphasized central area, having a round, square or polygonal ground plan.

In Ancient Greece, the circular plan was used for temples and tombs, and in the Christian era for BAPTISTRIES and sepulchral chapels. In BYZANTINE ARCHITECTURE, churches were often centrally planned. In the Baroque period, the central and longitudinal plan was sometimes combined.

Chamfer

ARRIS, or a piece of stone or wood cut at an angle of 45°.

Chancel

Area in which the ALTAR is placed and reserved for the officiating clergy, usually separated by a screen or railings. CHOIR.

Chantry

Small chapel attached to, or within, a church, endowed for the singing or saying of masses for the soul of the founder.

Chapter-House

Place of assembly, in England often polygonal in plan, attached to a monastery, cathedral, collegiate or other church, and normally used for the transaction of business by the monks or clergy.

Charterhouse

MONASTERY

Chequer-board Motif

ORNAMENT

Chevet

APSE, surrounded by an AMBULATORY from which a ring of chapels radiate, which is either circular or polygonal. Common in France. An English example can be seen in Westminster Abbey.

Chevron

ORNAMENT

Chimney-breast

Wall projecting into a room enclosing the fireplace and flue.

Chimney-piece

Decorative framework round the fireplace. Mantelpiece.

Chinoiserie

Style incorporating Chinese, or supposed Chinese, elements, and a particular manifestation of ROCOCO decoration.

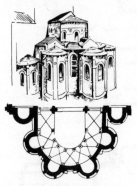

ambulatory of the choir with radiating chapels.

Choir

1. Area reserved for choristers;
2. CHANCEL, the term commonly used with reference to cathedrals and COLLEGIATE CHURCHES.

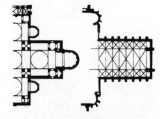

choir—round termination
choir—rectangular termination

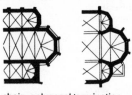

choir—polygonal termination

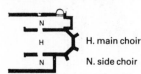

H. main choir

N. side choir

communicating side choirs

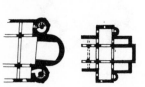

choir—retracted   choir—staggered

choir—trefoil

choir—Early Christian screen
with ambos

choir—screen

choir—stalls

Choir Screen

Barrier in a church
separating the area reserved
for clergy and choristers
from that of the laity. In
Early Christian churches, a
low stone parapet or screen,

occasionally incorporating the AMBOS. In the Middle Ages screens became much larger; they often encircle the whole CHOIR and may bear sculpture on the side facing the ambulatory.

Choir Stall

Seating for the choir and clergy, often richly carved. MISERICORD

Churrigueresque

Spanish Baroque style of decoration created by Jose Churriguera (1665—1725). Its apparently disorganised, overladen and sumptuous piling up of overall surface ornament may be compared to the Spanish late Gothic PLATERESQUE style.

Ciborium

1. Canopy resting on pillars, over an ALTAR, BALDACCHINO;
2. Container for the Eucharist, with a lid which, in Gothic examples, may be in the form of a spire.

Cinquefoil
ORNAMENT

Cistercian Architecture

Austere, markedly simple manifestation of Romanesque and Early Gothic architecture. The Cistercian Order, founded in Burgundy in 1098 by Robert of Molesme, eventually had almost 600 churches in Europe, based on the models of the mother abbeys, Clairvaux and Morimond (founded 1115). West fronts generally have no towers, and rarely have crossings; NAVES are commonly flat roofed.

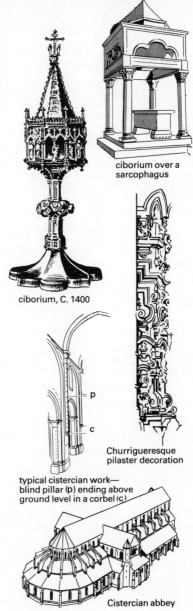

ciborium over a sarcophagus

ciborium, C. 1400

Churrigueresque pilaster decoration

typical cistercian work— blind pillar (p) ending above ground level in a corbel (c)

Cistercian abbey

97

cloisters

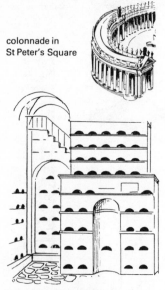

colonnade in
St Peter's Square

columbarium in a Roman
catacomb

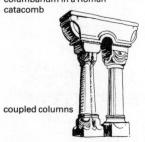

coupled columns

Clerestory
Upper wall of a hall or church, above the roof of the AISLES, pierced with windows which admit light to the central part of the building.

Cloister
MONASTERY

Cluny
Town near Macon in France celebrated for its Benedictine abbey which became the source of a monastic reform which dominated Western Europe and led to the erection of many elaborate Romanesque and later Gothic abbey buildings. The Cluniac Order was founded in 910 by Bernard of Cluny.

Coffer
CAISSON

Collegiate Church
Church endowed for a chapter, but with no bishop's see.

Colonnade
Row of COLUMNS supporting an ENTABLATURE.

Columbarium
1. Dove-cote or pigeon-cote;
2. Roman and Early Christian burial place, especially in the catacombs; because of lack of space, urns containing ashes were placed in numerous small cavities in the wall, which had the appearance of a dove-cote.

Column
1. Cylindrical, sometimes tapering, member erected

vertically as a support. In Classical architecture it is composed of BASE, SHAFT and CAPITAL. ORDERS;
2. Vertical member standing in isolation as a monument.

Concrete

Sand, water and rubble (usually stone or brick) bound with a mortar or cement to make a compact slurry, which hardens quickly in the air. It was used extensively by the Romans and in BYZANTINE ARCHITECTURE. Because of its tensile weakness now mostly used with steel, net or rod reinforcement.

Confessional

Box or stall for confessions. Since C 1600, generally a tripartite wooden structure with a seat for the priest in the central section, separated from the kneeling confessants whose confessions he hears alternately.

Console

BRACKET; in classical architecture, supported on VOLUTES.

Contrapposto

(Italian=counterpoise). The relationship of contrasted masses. More particularly, the representation of the equilibrium maintained in a standing human figure between forces tending to hold him erect and those tending to drag him down. The positioning and movement of the limbs are fixed through the careful mutual positioning of the temporarily stationary leg

and the free-moving one.

confessional

carved consoles— German C 1560

stone console

contrapposto line—Rococo 18th C—indicates movement away from the original axis of knees, hips, shoulders and eyes. This central line is maintained only by clothing. S. support leg

antique classical cornice

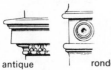

antique vault cornice   **rondel**

Gothic cornice

Gothic dripstone

Gothic base-moulding

chamfered cornice

Corbel

Support projecting from wall face, usually carved or moulded, supporting a beam or roof truss.

Corbelling

Succession of MASONRY or brick courses, each projecting beyond the one below it, designed as support.

Corbel Table

Projecting course of MASONRY, resting on a series of CORBELS.

Cornice

Crowning member of a Classical ENTABLATURE. Also any moulded projection framing a wall, door, window etc.

Crenellation

Openings of the indented parapet of a battlement. The raised parts are called MERLONS.

Crocket

ORNAMENT.

Cross

In Christian symbolism the following types occur:

1. Greek Cross (4 arms of equal length);
2. Roman Cross (crux immissa);
3. St Anthony's Cross (crux commissa);
4. St Peter's Cross (Peter was reputedly crucified head downwards);
5. St Andrew's Cross (symbolising the position in which Andrew was crucified);
6. Yoke Cross;
7. Cross of Lorraine (doubled);
8. Ansate Cross (crux ansata, originally Egyptian life-giving symbol));
9. Papal Cross (the three cross-beams symbolise priestly, doctrinal and pastoral offices);
10. Cross of Constantine (Christian monogram, first adopted by Constantine, from the Greek letters X (=Chi) and P (Rho), the initial letters of the word CHRistus, interlaced and crossed);
11. Russian Cross;

12. Re-duplicating Cross (the ends of each member are made into additional crosses);
13. Cross Potent (crook-shaped and familiar in heraldry);
14. Anchor Cross (cross motif in heraldry);
15. Clover-leaf Cross (croix botannee, treflee in heraldry);
16. Maltese Cross;
17. Tree Cross (Tree of Life, with leaves, buds, fruit; or double-branched without twigs).

The inscription INRI often found on representations of the Crucifixion stands for Iesus Nazarenus Rex Iudaeorum, Jesus of Nazareth, King of the Jews.

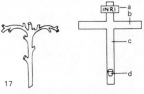

cross forms
a. inscription tablet; b. cross beam; c. pillar of cross; d. suppedaneum

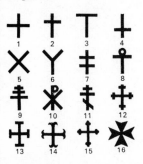

Crossing

Square or rectangular space formed at the intersection of NAVE, CHANCEL and TRANSEPTS in a cruciform church. The crossing sometimes provided the unit of measurement, or MODULE, for the whole church, particularly in Romanesque structures. It was often surmounted by a crossing tower.

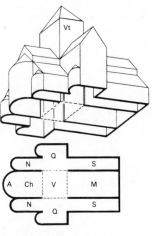

crossing: schematic representation of crossing and crossing tower of a basilica with Benedictine choir, with no regard to arcades of main building
V. crossing
Vt. crossing tower
Q. transept
Ch. choir
A. apse
N. side choir with side apse
M. nave
S. aisles

crypt

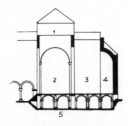

crypt beneath Romanesque church (longitudinal cross- section)

1. tower over crossing
2. crossing
3. choir
4. apse
5. crypt

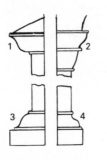

cyma—1=recta; 2=reversa; 3=reversa; 4=recta

Crow-step Gable

Gable with step-like projections on the sloping sides. Also called Corbie-step gable.

Crypt

Developed from the Early English Confessio, the burial place of a saint beneath the altar. Later, a partly or wholly subterranean area, almost always under the choir, for the preservation of relics, or as a burial chamber for saints and honoured citizens. Occasionally burial chambers were in one or several intersecting tunnels (tunnel crypts). From Italy in the 9th C. came hall crypts: they are vaulted, usually divided longitudinally by two ARCADES, and sometimes extend as far as the CROSSING. To give added height, the choir may be raised above the level of the NAVE. UNDERCROFT.

Cupola

Domed roof over a circular, square or polygonal space, also its ceiling.

Cusp

Projecting point between two arcs or FOILS in Gothic TRACERY

Cyma Recta

Double-curve MOULDING, of which the upper curve is concave and the lower convex; ogee moulding.

Cyma Reversa

Double-curve MOULDING, of which the upper curve is convex and the lower concave; ogee moulding.

Cymatium

The topmost member of a CORNICE generally in the form of a CYMA RECTA or CYMA REVERSA.

Dado

Lower part of a wall marked by a MOULDING and often of a different surface. In Classical architecture the part of the PEDESTAL between the base and CORNICE.

Dais

Raised platform at the end of a Medieval hall.

Dipteral

Temple with a double PERISTYLE.

Distyle

PORTICO with two columns.

Dog-tooth

Early English ornamental motif, consisting of a succession of pyramidal forms.

Dome

Vaulting of a round, square or polygonal area in the form of a hemisphere or semi-ellipse. The transition from a polygonal basic shape to the rounded form of the dome is achieved through PENDENTIVES. These are spherical concave triangles and are used in two ways:
1. The circular base of the dome circumscribes the polygon, the pendentives becoming integral parts of the dome itself;
2. The circular base of the dome is inscribed within the polygon, the pendentives becoming self-supporting parts of the construction. Between pendentives and dome, a cylindrical DRUM is usually in evidence, which may also be pierced with windows. Occasionally, the dome is crowned with an opening for light or a small crowning structure

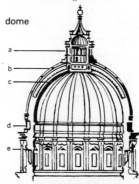

dome

two-skin dome, early Baroque, 16th century

    a. lanterns
    b. external masonry wall
    c. internal wall with stairs
    d. roof parapet
    e. drum

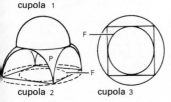

cupola 1

cupola 2   cupola 3

    H. suspension structure
    F. base
    P. pendentive
    F. base
    F. base

dormer rooms and gables

drapery

misericord showing a drolerie

called a lantern. Large domes are often built double-shelled, having an inner space and an outer protective skin.

Alternatively SQUINCHES, a series of concentric arches built across the corner of a square or polygon, can support a dome.

Donjon
KEEP or central fortress of a castle

Dormer
Windows projecting from the roof slope, usually with an independent covering.

Dripstone
Projecting MOULDING over an arch, doorway or window to throw off rainwater; label moulding, hood moulding.

Drapery
1. The effective arrangement of the folds, etc. of material, vestments, etc. in sculpture and painting; it demanded careful study before the artist began work;
2. The hanging of curtains, tapestries, etc.

Drolerie
ORNAMENT

Drum
Circular, square or polygonal wall supporting a CUPOLA or DOME.

Dwarf Gallery
GALLERY, usually arcaded, used externally on German and Italian Romanesque churches.

b dwarf gallery

Egg and Dart
Alternating oval and arrow-head motifs used to enrich MOULDINGS.

Elevation
Drawing which shows any one front of a building; also any such face itself.

Empire Style
Phase of Neo-Classicism which began under Napoleon Bonaparte and spread after 1804 from Paris to the rest of Europe. Its characteristics were the division of interior walls into strictly defined compartments and a sparing use of Romano-Egyptian ornamentation (sphinx, lyre, meander, torch etc).

Engaged Column
COLUMN partially built into a wall.

Entablature
In the Classical Orders, the group of horizontal elements, ARCHITRAVE, CORNICE and FRIEZE, supported by a COLUMN.

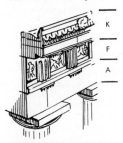

entablature of Greek Doric temple

A. architrave
F. decorated frieze with metopes
K. cornice

Entasis
Swelling of the Classical COLUMN SHAFT which counteracts the optical illusion of concavity of a straight-sided column.

empire style—table leg, chair and bronze vase

Entresol
Intermediate storey between two floors.

Epitaph
Inscription on a tomb or monument in honour of the dead. Memorials to the dead in the form of plaques came into existence in the 14th C.

Estrade
Raising of the floor by one or several steps, e.g. in front of a throne, altar or monument.

Exedra
1. In Classical architecture the PORTICO of a gymnasium reserved for disputation;
2. Vestibule of a private house;

3. Externally projecting PORCH, chapel or wall recess.

Facade

Face of a building, but usually the principal front. In English usage the main facade of a major church is generally described as the west front.

facade of Romanesque house

Fanlight

Fan-shaped, semicircular or elliptical window above a door, especially characteristic of Georgian and American Colonial architecture. Nowadays loosely applied to any type of window over a door.

Fan Vault

Fan-like effect in VAULTING produced by inverted concave cones overlaid with RIBS of the same length and curvature, characteristic of the final phase of Gothic in England. King's College Chapel, Cambridge, and Henry VII Chapel, Westminster Abbey, offer magnificent examples.

Fenestration

Manner in which the windows of a building are disposed.

Feretory

Shrine for relics, generally behind the high altar. Also a chapel for a shrine.

Festoon

ORNAMENT

Fillet

Narrow flat band between two MOULDINGS, also known as a listel. Also the vertical space between the flutes of a COLUMN or PILASTER.

Finial

Crowning feature of a pinnacle, spire, GABLE or PEDIMENT. Also applied to the carved tops of bench-ends (pews) in churches.

Flambeau
ORNAMENT

Flamboyant
ORNAMENT

Flèche
Slender, usually wooden, spire rising from the RIDGE of a church roof.

Fluting
Grooves in Classical COLUMNS or PILLARS which allow them to appear slimmer and more resilient. In a Doric COLUMN, the 22 grooves are separated by sharp ARRISES, while the fluting of an Ionic column is divided by 24 flat FILLETS.

Flying Buttress
BUTTRESS

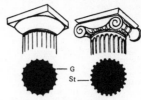

fluting: Doric (L) Ionic (R)
G. arris fluting St. web fluting

Foil
Small arc openings in Gothic TRACERY, separated by CUSPS. Hence trefoil, quatrefoil, multifoil, etc.

Foliated
Carved with leaf ornament.

Font
Stone, bronze or wooden basin, containing baptismal water, often decorated with biblical themes.

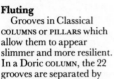

fleche

font—bronze

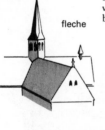

finial; Gothic

font

Fortalice

Originally a fortress. Subsequently used to describe a small fort or fortification.

Fountain

A place where water is projected out or up with some force, either by gravity or forced by a pump. Since the earliest times, the public watering places with decorative water-spouts have been a focal point in city planning. In Roman antiquity, fountains were often set in NYMPHAEA. Early Christian builders usually set one in the middle of the ATRIUM or CLOISTER. In the 16th/17th centuries the aqueduct fountain (e.g., Fontana di Trevi) developed on a vast monumental scale in Rome and was adapted in the rest of Europe and in North America.

Fret

Ornamental pattern of repeated combinations of straight lines meeting at right angles, e. g. (Greek) key pattern.

Frieze

1. Middle section of the ENTABLATURE, between the ARCHITRAVE and the CORNICE;
2. Decorative band on a wall. ORNAMENT.

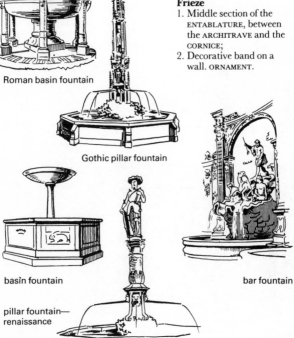

Roman basin fountain

Gothic pillar fountain

basin fountain

pillar fountain—
renaissance

bar fountain

Gable

Triangular upper part of a wall at the end of a ridged roof, in Classical architecture known as the PEDIMENT. Also the ornamental triangular form surmounting windows and doors.

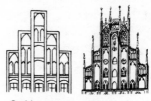

Gothic crow-step gable

Galilee

Vestibule or NARTHEX of a church enclosing the PORCH usually at the west end.

gable and scrollwork

Gallery

1. Covered passage, partly open at the sides. COLONNADE;
2. Long, narrow passage in the thickness of the walls or supported by CORBELS, open towards the interior of a building. TRIBUNE.
3. Platform or balcony supported by COLUMNS or BRACKETS increasing the seating space, as in a THEATRE;
4. Corridor;
5. Room or building for the exhibition of works of art.

galilee, narthex

genuine gallery   pseudo gallery or triforum   mock gallery

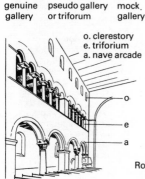

o. clerestory
e. triforium
a. nave arcade

o
e
a

bar gallery

Romanesque gallery: 10th C

109

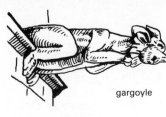

gargoyle

gallery in Gothic ambulatory

imperial gallery with
opening to ground floor

royal gallery on cathedral facade

Gargoyle

Water spout, projecting
rainwater clear of the wall
surface, often in the shape of
a grotesque human or
animal figure.

Garland
FESTOON

Georgian

Term applied to Late
Renaissance architecture in
England from the accession
of George I (1715) to the
death of George IV (1830).
Although the style evolved
considerably during the
period, it was characterized
throughout by a generally
restrained Classicism, which
drew its inspiration from
Palladio and the so-called
Neo-Palladians, while
initially owing much to
Dutch influence.

Giant Order
PILASTER or COLUMN which
extends over more than one
storey of a building.

Gilding

Applying a gold surface
to, usually, wooden statues,
both to conserve and to
decorate them.

Gloriette

Eye-catcher, ornamental
building.

Golden Section

A proportion which has
exercised the minds of
theorists since the fifteenth
century. If a line is cut, the
smaller part bears the same
relation to the larger as the
larger does to the whole, i. e.
the line C(=summa) is
divided into a small part A
(=minor) and a greater part
B (=major), so that they are

in the ratio A:B=B:C. As a rule of thumb 2:3=3:5=5:8=8:13 and so on. It is far less commonly applied than is generally believed.

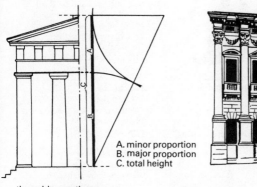

A. minor proportion
B. major proportion
C. total height

the golden section

giant order

gloriette

Gothic gable

Gothic Gable

Decorated GABLE over Gothic WINDOWS and PORTALS filled with TRACERY and topped with CROCKETS or a FINIAL.

Gothic Revival

Principally a revival style of the 19th C. in Britain with beginnings in the 18th C. Romantic interest in the Middle Ages. Churches were built in imitation of Medieval structures and later town halls, public buildings, railway stations and domestic buildings. Similar stylistic revivals occurred in other European countries and in North America.

Grid

Regular geometric basis for the plan of a building, in which the lines of the grid coincide with the main walls and the crossing points with main supports.

111

Gothic revival—London,
Albert memorial

Gothic revival

Lubeck, Marienkirche,
brick gothic: 13-14th. c.

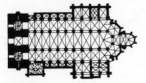

Gristaille

(Fr. grey painting).
Painting in grey shades of
colour, sometimes used for
delicately simulated
representations of statues
and stucco, but in building
principally applied to
medieval 'staining' in grey
monochrome of window glass.

Groin, Groin Vault
VAULTING

Grotesque

Fanciful or bizarre
decoration composed of
animal and human forms
and foliage. Used by Roman
mural painters, evidence of
this type of ornamentation
was discovered in grottoes
(hence the name) in the
High Renaissance and it
was much imitated.

Guilloche

Ornament of
symmetrically interlacing or
plaited bands, used
especially on MOULDINGS.

Half-timbering

Method of construction
allowing the weight of the
walls to be carried by the
wooden framework, instead
of by load-bearing walls. In
a half-timbered building,
the frame is filled in with
plaster, brick, stone, wattle
and daub, etc.

Hall Church

Church with AISLES of the
same height as the NAVE (as
distinct from a BASILICA).
There is no CLERESTORY, so
the high side windows
illuminate the nave.
Common in 13th and
14th C, particularly in
Westphalia, but also in
Southern France, Holland
and Italy. A pseudo-basilica
is a hall church with
elevated nave and basilican
roof formation, but without
a clerestory.

Hammer-beam

A timber roof TRUSS
projecting from the top of a
wall, used as a BRACKET and

112

not carried across the space.
Peculiar to English late
Gothic and Tudor constructions.

hatchment

Hatchment

Escutcheon; shield or
tablet with armorial
bearings, often hung in
churches.

Header

BRICKWORK

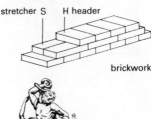

stretcher S   H header

brickwork

Hellenistic Art

Greek art from the time of
Alexander the Great until
Augustus (323—14 BC).
Subservience to an
exclusively national Greek
art was relinquished in
favour of the aspiration to a
universal culture by
consciously drawing on
oriental influences as well.
Architecture and sculpture
lost their classical serenity in
favour of a wealth of
naturalistic decoration.
Hellenistic Art was of the
greatest significance to
Roman Art.

Hellenistic art

hall church

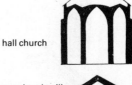

pseudo—basilica
—hall church

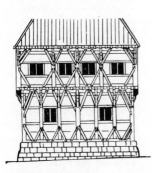

half-timbering

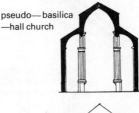

hall—church

herm

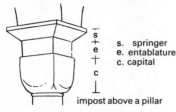

s. springer
e. entablature
c. capital

impost above a pillar

impost with hirsauer
ornament

incrustation—
marble

Helm Roof
ROOF

Herm
PEDESTAL, tapering
towards the base and
carrying the sculptured
head or three-quarter length
figure of a man (or woman).
Also known as a Term.

Herringbone work
Stone or brick laid in a
zigzag pattern as paving or
in the panels of HALF-
TIMBERED buildings.

Hip
External angle formed by
the intersection of the
sloping sides of a roof.

Hypocaust
1. Underground room or
   flue in the Roman system
   of central heating;
2. Room heated from
   beneath.

Hypotrachelium
Lower part or neck of a
CAPITAL; in the Doric ORDER
the groove between the neck
of the capital and the SHAFT.

Impost
BRACKET or projection
from the wall from which
the ARCH springs. Usually
with a MOULDING.

Incrustation
(L. crusta=edge). Inlay
(or overlay) of coloured
stones in woods or semi-
precious materials (e. g.
mother-of-pearl) used to
embellish wall and floor
surfaces. Its high period was
classical Antiquity.
BYZANTINE art, Italian from
the Middle Ages to the
Baroque.

Intarsia

Mosaic of different coloured woods, a popular form of decoration in Italy in the Renaissance for the wall panels of small rooms and for CHOIR STALLS.

Intercolumniation

Space between two COLUMNS, measured at the lower part of the column. Vitruvius established five principal ratios.

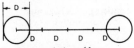

intercolumniation of four pillar's diameter D (araeostyle)

Jambs

Side of a doorway, or other opening supporting a beam or arch. If the opening is glazed, the part of the jamb outside the glazing is known as the reveal.

Jetty

Projecting floor-joist in a TIMBER-FRAMED building.

Joist

One of a number of parallel beams upon which floor-boards or ceiling-laths are laid.

Jube

French equivalent of the English ROOD SCREEN

Jugendstil

German variant of ART NOUVEAU with which it shared the principal characteristics. The movement derived its name from the Munich periodical 'Jugend' (Youth). More a fashion in decoration than an architectural style.

Keep

DONJON. Inner tower of a castle.

Keystone

Central wedge-shaped stone or VOUSSOIR of an ARCH, often ornamented.

King-post

Central vertical post of a roof TRUSS extending from the tie-beam to the RIDGE.

Labyrinth

Geometrical patterning in dark and light stone in the floor of some, mainly Gothic, cathedrals. The faithful moved along the maze on their knees, from the periphery to the centre, as penitents. The unravelled length of the labyrinth at Chartres is 250 metres.

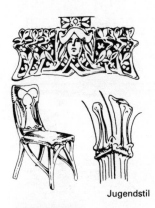

Jugendstil

labyrinth—1

labyrinth—2

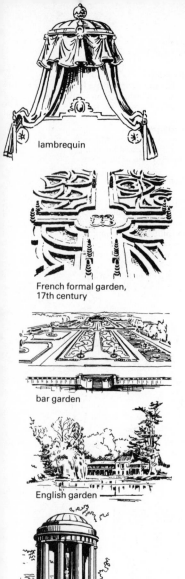

lambrequin

French formal garden,
17th century

bar garden

English garden

gloriette

Lacunar CAISSON

Lady Chapel
Chapel dedicated to the
Virgin Mary, usually
situated to the east of the
high altar. Used for private
prayer and small congregations.

Lambrequin
Drapery above a window,
bed or door. The
lambrequin was sometimes
imitated in STUCCO or stone.

Landscape Architecture
Principal historical types
of gardens were:
1. The formal, geometrically
   designed garden, an early
   example of which was the
   roof or hanging gardens of
   Babylon. From the Greek
   and Roman gardens, with
   statuary, pavilions and
   seats, evolved the
   Renaissance gardens of
   Italy and France,
   culminating in the
   grandiose schemes of Le
   Nôtre and his imitators in
   the Baroque period.
   Fountains and cascades,
   GLORIETTES, belvederes,
   ORANGERIES, NYMPHAEA
   and other small buildings
   were often incorporated
   in their design;
2. The English landscape
   garden, which spread to
   the European continent in
   the 18th C, presented a
   blend of nature and
   artifice. The seemingly
   casual asymmetry of the
   design was enlivened by
   buildings and monuments
   with particular, often
   romantic, associations;
   artificial ruins (the past),
   Gothic hermitages
   (solitude), peasants'
   cottages (simplicity),
   Chinese bridges and
   pagodas (exotic lands).

Lantern
DOME

Lectern
Sloping book-support on a stand for the Gospel or Epistle.

Lenten Veil
Large linen cloth divided into square panels and painted, printed or otherwise worked with the scenes of Christ's Passion. During Lent it was suspended between CHANCEL and NAVE.

Lesene
Plain PILASTER without BASE or CAPITAL.

Lierne
Short RIB connecting main ribs of VAULT.

Lighting
Before the use of electricity, lighting was provided by the burning of liquid or solid fat. The principal forms of light-holders were:

1. Candelabrum; Standing candle-holder, since Antiquity found in numerous forms such as the seven-branched Jewish 'menora' (found in Christian churches as a symbol of the fulfilment of the Old Testament);
2. Chandelier: Branched candle-holder suspended from ceiling. Sometimes in the shape of a wheel, with symbolic towers and city gates representing Jerusalem in the Romanesque period; sometimes in the form of a crown, or as a shaft with radiating arms;

eagle lectern; Gothic   lectern

lenten veil

3. Wall sconce: Single or branched holder attached to the wall, usually with a reflecting panel of metal or mirror-glass. ▶

candelabra

117

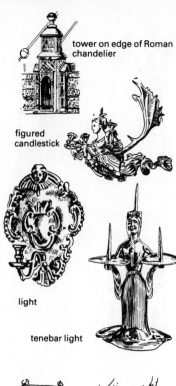

tower on edge of Roman chandelier

figured candlestick

light

tenebar light

linenfold on wooden chair— recessed portal

Linenfold

Wood panelling of the 15th and 16th centuries carved to resemble linen folded vertically. Also seen on furniture of the same period.

Lintel

Horizontal member which spans an opening.

Listel

FILLET

Loggia

ARCADE. Open on at least one side. Part of a building or a separate building.

Louis Quatorze

French style of decorative art at the time of the Sun King, Louis XIV (1643—1715). The description is applied not to architecture, but to the entire vocabulary of ornament devised by the versatile Charles Le Brun (1619—90)

Louis Quinze

Style current in France during the reign of Louis XV (1715—74), broadly applicable to decoration and the applied arts. In architecture, the ornamental exuberance of le style Louis XV gave way to a more restrained and stricter Classical elegance long before Louis XV died, while the style of the early years of his reign is described as REGENCE, not to be confused with English REGENCY.

loggia

Louis Seize

The transition style from ROCOCO to NEO-CLASSICISM in France before and during the reign of Louis XVI (1774—92). It denotes a quiet, strictly symmetrical clarity of form.

Louis Seize window

Lozenge
ORNAMENT

Lucarne

Small opening or DORMER.

Lunette

Semicircular window or panel.

Mannerism

In architecture, the term has come to be applied to the work of certain highly accomplished architects in Italy during the period of transition from the High Renaissance to the Baroque (c 1530—1600). By this time the architectural idiom of Classical Rome was fully understood, and architects were thus tempted to exploit their own scholarship in free interpretations of the vocabulary of Classical architecture. Outstanding examples of Mannerism can be seen in buildings by Michelangelo and Giulio Romano.

Mansard
ROOF TYPES

Marble

Crystalline limestone used in building and sculpture since Ancient times. In Baroque decoration marble is often imitated in painted wood or STUCCO. It is found in many European mountainous areas in hundreds of shades and colours. White marble has been preferred since Classical times. The Greek varieties were famous: the marble of Mount Pentelicon (bluish) and Parian marble (blue-white); also the Italian Carrara marble from the quarries of Tuscany, which Michelangelo used.

Mask
ORNAMENT

Masonry

Stonework. In Britain building in stone was encouraged by the Romans, but after their departure in the 5th C the practice was discontinued. It was revived with the emergence of the Gothic style. Particularly in GEORGIAN architecture brick FACADES may have a dressing of stone. The principal types of masonry walling are:

1. Rubble. Random rubble walls are built of stones of irregular shape and size and not coursed. In coursed random rubble walls, the stones of irregular shape and size are arranged in parallel layers. In Classical architecture large, irregular stonework is known as Cyclopean;
2. ASHLAR. Wall stones of regular dimensions laid in courses with thin joints.

random rubble masonry   coursed

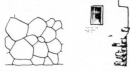

cyclopean masonry   rustic quoins

rustication

rusticated stone with
squared end

dressed stone with
chamfered edge

stone mason's marks

Mason's Lodge
   Workshop and place of
rest of Medieval
stonemasons connected with
the particular building work
in progress. Freemasonry
developed from these craft
organisations.

Mason's Mark
   Identification of the
master stonemason.

Mausoleum
   Stately place of burial.
The term derives from the
tomb of Mausolus at
Halicarnassus, one of the
'Seven Wonders of the
World.'

Meander
ORNAMENT

Medallion
   Painting or sculpture in a
round or oval frame.

Merlon
   Raised part of
battlements.

Metope
   Space, plain or decorated,
between the TRIGLYPHS on a
classical FRIEZE.

Mezzanine
   Intermediate storey
between two floors.

Minster
   Originally the complete
monastic establishment,
later only the monastery
church; the name of a
cathedral or principal
church, e. g. York.

Misericord
   Hinged seat in the CHOIR
STALLS with a BRACKET,
often grotesquely or

humorously carved on the underside, to provide support for the standing occupant.

Roman mausoleum

misericord

Modern Architecture

Currently the appellation of an architecture which developed in the late 19th C in the USA and Europe. Characterised by simplicity and the use of machine-made elements. Its principal masters are Louis Sullivan and the Chicago School Architects in the USA, Auguste Perret and Le Corbusier in France, Walter Gropius and Mies van der Rohe in Germany, Aalto in Finland.

medallion

mezzanine

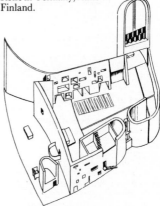
modern architecture—Ronchamp pilgrimage church

metope relief

Module

1. Unit of proportion, being the diameter, or half the diameter of a column at its base (INTER-COLUMNIATION) from which the proportions of an Order, or an entire building, are calculated. A module of half the diameter is divided into 30 parts or minutes, and of the whole diameter into 60 minutes;
2. Used by the building industry to describe any basic unit of measurement.

Monastery

In 529 St Benedict founded a monastery at Monte Cassino, in Southern Italy, that was to serve as the model for Benedictine monasteries throughout Europe. A typical Cistercian monastery (the Order was founded in 1098) had an open, rectangular court round which ran the CLOISTERS, deriving from the PERISTYLE of ancient Classical residences, with the lavabo, and the other rooms ranged around them: the church usually lay to the north, the CHAPTER-HOUSE serving as an assembly room; the REFECTORY was a dining hall, the parlatorium a main living room, the dormitory for sleeping and the monks' cells for private prayer and meditation, or sometimes as private rooms where there was no common dormitory. While the Benedictine monks liked to build on mountains and the Cistercians in the valleys, the mendicant orders settled in or near towns, as they saw their office less as one of meditation than of the 'cure of souls'. The Carthusians lived in separate small houses disposed round a large cloister. Their monasteries came to be called Charterhouses. The castles of the Teutonic Knights and other Military Orders served equally as their monasteries. Baroque monastic building came nearer to palace building in its spacious and lavish appurtenances.

Carthusian monastery

Monopteral

CELLA, generally circular embraced by a circular COLONNADE.

Mouchette

Dagger motif in Gothic TRACERY.

Moulding

Horizontal or vertical band, either projecting or recessed, usually at the point where two planes or elements meet. Each architectural style has its characteristic forms of moulding, such as the egg and tongue or bead and reel mouldings of Classical Antiquity (ORNAMENT). A string-course is a moulding or projecting row of stone or brick extending horizontally across a FACADE.

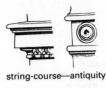

string-course—antiquity

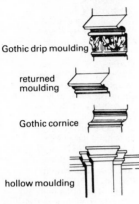

Gothic drip moulding

returned moulding

Gothic cornice

hollow moulding

Mullion
WINDOW

Mutule
Projecting square block above the TRIGLYPH on the SOFFIT of a Doric CORNICE.

Nailhead
Early English MOULDING of closely repeating small pyramidal studs.

obelisk—crowning cornice

Naos
CELLA. Principal chamber of a Greek temple housing the statue of the deity.

Narthex
Arcaded PORCH or antechurch, originally the appointed place of penitents. GALILEE.

Nave
Main body or central area of a church.

Necking
Convex MOULDING at the top of the SHAFT of a COLUMN, beneath the CAPITAL.

Newel
Post on which a WINDING STAIRCASE centres; in a square staircase, the angle pillar.

Nosing
Rounded projecting edge of a tread on a stair.

Nymphaeum
'Temple of the nymphs' or garden PAVILION.

Obelisk
High, rectangular stone PILLAR, tapering from bottom to top and ending in a pyramid.

Octagon
Building of eight sides.

Oeil de Boeuf
BULL'S EYE WINDOW, an oval or round window, often with glazing bars radiating from a small circular pane.

Ogee Arch
Pointed ARCH of double curvature; convex below, concave above.

123

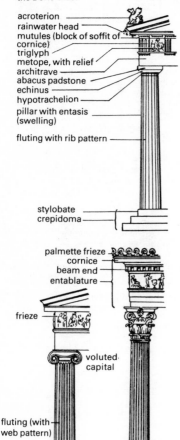

the Doric order

- acroterion
- rainwater head
- mutules (block of soffit of cornice)
- triglyph
- metope, with relief
- architrave
- abacus padstone
- echinus
- hypotrachelion
- pillar with entasis (swelling)
- fluting with rib pattern
- stylobate
- crepidoma

- palmette frieze
- cornice
- beam end
- entablature
- frieze
- voluted capital
- fluting (with web pattern)
- base
- torus

construction of Ionic, and Corinthian columns

Orangery
 Garden building with large windows for the growing of oranges.

Oratory
1. Chapel for private devotions;
2. Church of the Congregation of the Fathers of the Oratory (constituted in 1564).

Orders
 Order in architecture comprises a COLUMN, usually with BASE, SHAFT and CAPITAL, the whole supporting an ENTABLATURE. The Greeks recognised three Orders: Doric, Ionic and Corinthian. The Romans added the Tuscan and Composite.
1. The Doric order first appeared in stone in the 7th C, BC, in Greece occupied by the Dorian invaders. Unique in having no BASE to the column, it is characterised by a strong contrast between the horizontal and vertical elements, with no gradual transition. The capital is plain; the shaft fluted;
2. The Ionic Order originated in the 6th C, BC, in Ionia (the coast of Asia Minor and the adjoining islands). Lighter, more elegant than the Doric, with slim, fluted columns, it is principally distinguished by the VOLUTES of its capital. It has an ATTIC BASE;
3. The Corinthian Order differs from the Ionic by the invention (5th C, BC) of the bell-shaped

ACANTHUS capital, from
which eight small volutes
or cauliculi emerge. The
shaft is generally fluted;
4. The Tuscan, the plainest
of the Orders, has a very
simple ENTABLATURE, an
unfluted shaft and a
capital not unlike the
Doric; however, the
column usually has a
base;
5. The Composite or Roman
Order combines the
volutes of the Ionic with
the acanthus of the
Corinthian on its capital,
and is thus the most
decorated. The shaft may
be fluted or plain.

oratory

Organ Loft
GALLERY in church or
concert hall to house the
organ.

Organ Screen
Ornamental screen
between NAVE and CHOIR,
upon which the organ is
sometimes placed in
cathedrals or other
important churches. The
elaborately decorated
'display' front of organs is
typical of Central European
Baroque.

Oriel Window
Corbelled-out BAY
WINDOW on an upper storey.

Orientation
Siting of a building in
relation to the points of the
compass. In Western
European churches, the
CHANCEL and altar are
usually placed at the east
end, so that the priest and
congregation face towards
the Holy Land and the
rising sun.

Ornament
Decorative motif; single
item of embellishment.
Ornament may be purely
decorative (e. g. rocaille,
astragal, arabesque) or used
as a dividing element (e. g.
STRAPWORK, TRACERY)—the
line between the two
functions cannot always be
sharply drawn, for a
decorative FRIEZE can at the
same time divide the
surface. The main forms are:
1. Geometric, e. g. zigzag,
meander, chequer-board;
2. Foliate, e. g. ACANTHUS;
3. Animal, e. g. bucranium;
4. Human, e.g. figured.

ornament—
meander, chien   ornament—courant,
                     antique

ornament— palmette

ornament— bucrania with garland

chien courant, wave pattern

ornament— astragal beading

ornament—wave pattern

ornament— cymatium

ornament— disc moulding

ornament— egg and dart

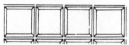

ornament—plate moulding

ornament— cymatium

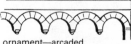

ornament—twisted roll

ornament— tongue frieze

ornament— dog's tooth

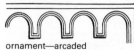

ornament—arcaded

ornament— dog's tooth

ornament—arcaded

ornament—indented

ornament—interlaced arches

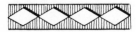

ornament—rhomboid

ornament—interlace

ornament—bead roll

ornament— diamond pattern

ornament
—chequerboard

17 ornament
—lunette

ornament— diamond pattern
archivolt

ornament—diamond pattern

ornament—foliate

ornament—foliate

ornament— bestiary

ornament
—trefoil

ornament
—quadrifoil

ornament
– cinquefoil

ornament
– hexafoil

ornament
– trefoil

ornament
– quadrifoil

ornament
– cinquefoil

ornament
—plurifoil

trefoil and interlace ornament

ornament
– geometric

ornament
– flamboyant,

ornament—rosette

ornament
—rosette

ornament
—waved rosette

127

tracery window ornament—

flamboyant— late Gothic 15th/16th C,
French and English origin

ornament
–green man

ornament
–grotesque
mask

ornament
–foliated
grotesque

ornament
–grotesque

ornament
–cartouche

ornament
–cartouche

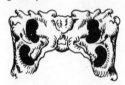

ornament—rocaille

ornament—arabesque

ornament—mauresque

ornament—rocaille

ornament—palmette acroterion

ornament—acanthus leaf

ornament—palmette acroterion

ornament – pine cone

ornament – crocket

ornament – crocket

ornament—garland

ornament—cross finial

ornament —fleur de lis

ornament—foliated arch

129

ornament—moulded rocaille border

ornament—strapwork

ornament—lisene; Romanesque

ornament— knife-carved

ornament—flambeau

ornament—drolerie

Overhang

Upper storey or storeys of a building, cantilevered over the ground floor. Common in Medieval half-timbered houses, especially in gabled street frontages.

Ovolo

ORNAMENT

Convex MOULDING used in Classical and Renaissance architecture ornamented with the egg and dart motifs.

Palladian Style

Architecture of the many disciples of Andrea Palladio (1508—80), most influential of Italian Renaissance architects, who worked mainly in Venice, the Veneto and the town of Vincenza, and set down his theories, based on close study of Ancient Roman remains, in his renowned work 'I quattro libri dell'architettura'. Palladianism was introduced to England by Inigo Jones in the early 17th C, but was not widely followed until a century later, when it was revived by Lord Burlington and became throughout most of the 18th C the English national style. Palladio was a strict and restrained interpreter of the Classical idiom, with a sense of harmonius splendour and grandeur, employing the GIANT ORDER to good effect.

Palmette

ORNAMENT.

Panelling

Lining of thin panels of wood for internal walls or doors. In early panelling the framing, of styles (vertical strips) and rails (horizontal strips), was a pronounced feature. LINENFOLD.

Pantile

Roof-tile of s-shaped section.

overhang of
an upper storey
and oriel window

pantile

Parclose

Screen enclosing a chapel (usually a CHANTRY) to separate it from the body of the church.

Patina

External film on copper and bronze, which appears eventually through oxidation and which is, nowadays, frequently artificially produced. Its green, brown or black colour is treasured as a mark of age.

Pavilion

1. In a garden, a small free-standing ornamental pleasure-house;
2. Projection, usually ornamental, rising from the centre and/or ends of a building.

pavilion

pediments

pendant

Pedestal
1. In Classical architecture, the BASE of a COLUMN;
2. Block, commonly a column, supporting a statue or urn.

Pediment
Triangular, sometimes ornamented, GABLE in a Classical building with a low-pitched roof. From the 16th C it occurred in broken and segmental as well as triangular form.

Peel or Pele Tower
Square, defensive tower built in the border counties of England and Scotland, especially.

Pendant
Elongated BOSS projecting downwards or suspended from the point of intersection of the ribs of a VAULT in late Gothic fan vaults or from the beams of a timbered roof.

Pendentive
Triangular curved surface formed between each pair of supporting arches in the construction of a DOME on a square base.

pendentive: H. suspension structure

Pergola
Covered walk combining stone, brick or trellis with climbing plants.

Peripteral
Temple surrounded by a single range of columns.

Peristyle
Range of columns surrounding a courtyard or building.

Perpendicular Style
Late stage of English Gothic (1350 to mid - 16th C). The name derives from the vertical line of its TRACERY in the wide, high windows. The fan vaulting associated with it is particularly striking.

Perpendicular traceried window

Mathematically exact perspective was only invented in the early Renaissance. The Baroque made use of perspective to simulate architectural effects, applying it in particular, with great virtuosity, to ceilings which appeared to extend into infinity.

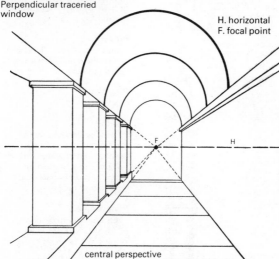

H. horizontal
F. focal point

central perspective

Perspective
Representation of three-dimensional space (length, breadth and depth) on a two-dimensional surface. Equally large objects are drawn gradually smaller in proportion to their increasing distance.

Piano Nobile
Principal floor of a Renaissance domestic building raised one storey above ground level and containing the reception rooms.

Pier
Broad column or small wall of solid masonry sustaining a structural load. In Gothic architecture a cluster of SHAFTS may be described as a compound pier.

'antique' perspective—
evangelist Matthew

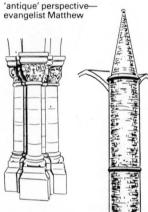

compound pier

masonry pier—
Gothic church

base of Gothic
compound pier

Pilaster
Rectangular column which projects a little from a wall, used to strengthen or divide the wall, carry an ARCHITRAVE or frame a PORTAL or window.

Pillar
Vertical support having a square, rectangular, polygonal or circular cross-section. (A COLUMN is always circular in section). Not necessarily conforming with any ORDER.

Pilotis
Posts or stilts standing on open ground and carrying a raised building.

Pine Cone
ORNAMENT

Piscina
Stone basin for liturgical use, usually in a niche near the altar and provided with a drain. Used for washing the consecrated vessels and the hands of the priest.

Plateresque
Ornate style of decoration of the Spanish late Gothic phase (16th C), resembling silverwork and characterised by a lavish use of ornamental motifs borrowed from Moorish and Renaissance sources.

Plinth
Lowest regular square or rectangular projecting member of the base of a COLUMN, PEDESTAL.

Porch
Covered entrance to a building

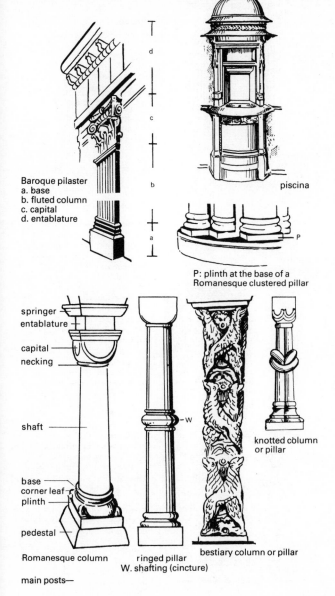

Baroque pilaster
a. base
b. fluted column
c. capital
d. entablature

piscina

P: plinth at the base of a
Romanesque clustered pillar

springer
entablature

capital
necking

shaft

base
corner leaf
plinth

pedestal

Romanesque column

main posts—

ringed pillar
W. shafting (cincture)

bestiary column or pillar

knotted column
or pillar

Roman portal

1. door lintel
2. arch bay (tympanum)
3. door pier
6. arch intrados, with archivolts

Gothic portal
4. door posts
5. jamb with carved jamb figures
6. arch intrados
7. openwork gablet
8. gable
9. porch frame

Gothic portal

portico

136

Portal
Imposing entrance

Renaissance portal

Portcullis
Heavy lattice grating of wood or iron, which slides in vertical grooves in the JAMBS of a gateway of a defended building.

Porte-cochere
Gateway, or passage through a building into a courtyard, large enough to admit a carriage.

Portico
Covered COLONNADE forming the main entrance of a building. If projecting, it is a PROSTYLE: if recessed, a prostyle in antis.

Presbytery
1. Part of a church, usually the eastern part of the CHANCEL, reserved for the clergy;
2. Clergy's dwelling

Profile
Section of a MOULDING or contour of a building.

Pronaos
Vestibule, enclosed by side walls and columns in front of the NAOS in temple architecture.

late Baroque portal

neo-classical portal

paradise portal

profile

Proportion

Mathematical relationship between the parts of a building, analogous to the proportions of the human body. In the Middle Ages, forms of proportions based on the square and its diagonal (adquadratum) or the equilateral triangle (adtriangulum) were commonly used.

Propylaeum

Entrance pavilion (usually columnar) to an enclosure, usually temple precincts, as at the Acropolis in Athens.

Prostyle

Having columns in front as in a PORTICO.

Pseudodipteral

Temple with DIPTERAL column-spacing, but without the inner range of columns.

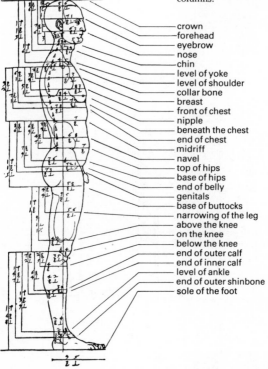

crown
forehead
eyebrow
nose
chin
level of yoke
level of shoulder
collar bone
breast
front of chest
nipple
beneath the chest
end of chest
midriff
navel
top of hips
base of hips
end of belly
genitals
base of buttocks
narrowing of the leg
above the knee
on the knee
below the knee
end of outer calf
end of inner calf
level of ankle
end of outer shinbone
sole of the foot

teaching plan of proportions. canon of the human body
—according to Dürer, 1528

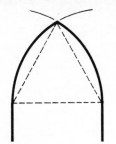

proportion—triangulation

propylaeum of acropolis

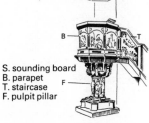

S. sounding board
B. parapet
T. staircase
F. pulpit pillar

pulpit: Renaissance

Pulpit
Raised, enclosed platform from which, in a church, a preacher delivers a sermon.

Pulpitum
Stone screen with gallery placed at the entrance to the choir of a major church and dividing it from the nave.
ROOD SCREEN.

Putto
Painted or carved representation of a naked (male) child.

putto

Rococo putto

eros figure

pylons; bar

Pylon

In ancient Egyptian architecture, truncated pyramidal towers flanking a temple gateway; and, more loosely, any high, isolated structure marking a boundary or used decoratively.

Quadriga

Greek war chariot, open at the back and drawn by four horses in line abreast. Used in Rome in chariot races and triumphal processions. Since the 4th C, BC, (Halicarnassus Mausoleum) employed as a decorative crowning motif on monuments.

Quatrefoil

ORNAMENT

Queen-post

One of the two upright timbers between the tie-beam and principal rafters of a roof-truss.

Re-Entrant

In fortifications, an inward-pointing angle (opposite of SALIENT)

Refectory

Dining-hall of MONASTERY.

Regence

Term applied to the art of Louis XV's minority (1715—23) in architecture, marked by decorative gaiety and elegance, especially of domestic interiors, rather than by structural innovation.

quadriga

Regency

Period in English history embracing the last decade of George III's reign and the subsequent ten years when the Prince Regent ruled as George IV, 1811—30. It was a time of extraordinary contrasts: on the one hand an immaculate Classical elegance; on the other, the most extreme eclecticism.

Relief

Sculpture carved out of a plane surface, but which remains perceptibly part of it. The main types, according to the degree of prominence of the figures, are:
1. Sunk relief; figures are incised deep into the surface and do not project;
2. Bas-relief or low relief; shallow relief;
3. Half relief;
4. High relief; figures stand out sharply from the surface.

Reredos
Screen or ornamental structure rising behind an ALTAR.

Respond
Engaged IMPOST usually supporting the end arch of an ARCADE.

Retable
Framework enclosing a picture or decorated panels behind an ALTAR and normally attached to it.

Return
Part of a wall, continuous moulding, frieze, etc, which turns away from the previous direction or recedes from the line of the front.

Revetment
Retaining wall built to hold back water, earth, etc. In areas adjoining the Baltic Sea, a projecting terraced revetment with steps replaces the garden of a house.

Rib
Projecting band of stone or brick which helps to support or ornament VAULTING.

Ridge
Horizontal line or member along the apex of a ROOF.

Ridge Rib
Secondary decorative or structural rib in VAULTING.

Rocaille
ORNAMENT. ROCOCO

Rococo
Style of the later years of the reign of Louis XIV, through the REGENCE to its full flowering in the middle years of Louis XV's reign, c 1740—50. In architecture it may be described as the superimposing of ornament of infinite, if often frivolous, invention upon strictly Classical forms. Originating in France, it spread throughout Europe.

Roll Moulding
MOULDING of semicircular or more than semicircular section.

Rood Loft
GALLERY carrying the 'rood' or crucifix, built above the ROOD SCREEN and sometimes used by minstrels.

Rood Screen
Partition between the CHOIR and the NAVE with one or more passages through it. Many were destroyed during the Reformation.

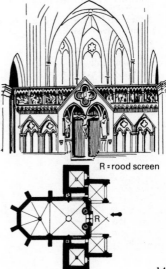

R = rood screen

141

Roof Types

1. Single pitch: roof over rectangular building, which slopes in one direction only;
2. Lean-to: with a single slope, normally against an adjoining wall;
3. Double pitch;
4. Hipped: a double pitched roof with sloped instead of vertical ends;
5. Half-hipped: the uppermost parts of the GABLE ends are inclined inwards towards the RIDGE;
6. Gabled: a double-pitched roof ending in a gable at either end;
7. Pyramid: square, rectangular or polygonal on plan, with sloping sides meeting at apex;
8. Mansard: named after the French architect Francois Mansart (1598—1668). A roof with double slope, the lower steeper and larger than the upper.
   A Gambrel roof is a slightly curved Mansard with ridge gable;
9. Saddleback: a gabled roof, but usually only when applied to tower roofs;
10. Helm: roof with four diamond-shaped faces resting between the gables. This type approximates to the Rhenish Helm of Central Europe, where the term Helm is applied to many kinds of tower roof, cone-shaped, pyramidal, domed;
11. North Light: presents a serrated outline and when, glazed, provides well-lit work areas.

Known as a Shed roof on the Continent;

12. Wagon: so called because of its resemblance to the stretched canvas covering of a wagon.

lean-to   saddleback

hipped   half-hipped

pavilion   mansard

north light   helm

onion   welsh bonnet   gabled steeple

rhomboidal   transverse

Rosette
ORNAMENT

Rotunda
1. Building or room that is circular or oval on plan and often domed;
2. DOME over part of a building.

rotunda

Roundel
  Round panel, especially of STAINED GLASS.

Rustication
MASONRY with recessed joints and usually a roughened surface.

sarcophagus

rustication

Roman voluted sarcophagus

Sacristy
  Room in a church where the vestments and sacred vessels are kept.

Salient
  Feature which juts outward. In fortifications, an outward-pointing angle.

Sarcophagus
TOMBS

Scaffolding Recesses
  Rectangular hole left in the MASONRY of Medieval churches to accommodate wooden scaffolding.

Scotia
  Concave MOULDING between the two TORUS mouldings at the base of a column.

Scroll Moulding
  Almost circular or semicircular MOULDING with a slight edge.

sacristy

Sculpture

Sculpture appears in connection with architecture in the form of RELIEFS and detached statuary. It is used to articulate parts of a building (HERM, CARYATID) or its functions (ACROTERION, GARGOYLE), as well as to embellish the building generally. Sculptures may be of the same material as the building itself (stone, timber, more rarely of brick) or they may be another material, such as bronze.

Sedilia

Seating arrangement, usually tripartite, frequently on the southern side of CHANCEL, on which the priest and his two deacons sit. In early Gothic churches, it was a recess in the wall, and only later did it become a carved wooden structure compatible with the CHOIR STALLS.

Severy

Bay or compartment in VAULTING.

Sgraffito

Wall-painting, in which variously coloured layers of plaster are deeply scratched so that the desired colour underneath is left visible.

Shaft

1. Body of a COLUMN between the base and capital;
2. Quarter, half or three-quarter small engaged column, for example, in a clustered pier supporting a VAULTING rib.

Skirting

Narrow horizontal member, generally a wooden board, along the bottom of an internal wall.

Soffit

Undersurface of an ARCH, ARCHITRAVE or other architectural feature.

sedilia

M | P | sgraffito
P. three-coloured plastering
M. masonry

shafts
a: principal shaft
b: secondary shaft

Sopraporta

Overdoor. A decorative framed panel painting or bas-relief placed above a door and usually forming part of the door-case.

Spandrel

In-fill panel between the arches of an ARCADE. Recently also used for the in-fill panel between the ribs of a curtain wall.

Spring, Springing

Point at which an ARCH rises from its support.

Squinch

Structural device, generally arched, placed across the angle of a square or polygon, thus increasing the number of load-bearing elements, in order to support a DOME or other superstructure.

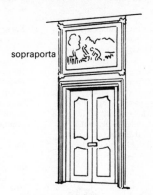

sopraporta

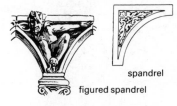

figured spandrel

spandrel

squinch

Stained Glass

Stained-glass windows are of Byzantine origin and became popular in the early Middle Ages, when a technique of painting on glass was supplemented by the mosaic effect of cutting out coloured glass pieces and mounting the whole composition in lead battens. From the building of St Denis onwards, stained-glass windows became a dominant feature of Gothic architecture.

The cartoon (full-size design of the artist) indicates the main outlines of the picture. From its lines, pieces of glass are cut out which are either stained (mosaic glass), or covered over with a thin, stained-glass layer (plated glass). Leaden rods, which are

145

soldered on at the points of contact, bind the pieces of glass. Horizontal storm bars (S) prevent displacement in high winds. These are connected to the window over vertically aligned bracing rods (B) and lead clasps (L) – wiring which is brazed on to the leaden frame outline and tied around the bracing rods.

stained glass

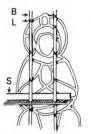

stained glass

B. bracing rods
L. lead clasps
S. storm bars

Stave Church

Wooden church, probably derived from the Nordic King's Hall. Named from the upright mast-like planks used in building the walls. Often crowned with dragons' heads and decorated with Viking animal ornamentation.

Stele

Stone with inscription. An upright stone slab, forming a tombstone or carrying an inscription.

Stilted Vault

VAULTING

Stoa

Greek PORTICO. Detached colonnade.

Stone

As building material, rock cut from natural deposits of sandstone, limestone (in crystalline form: marble) or granite, and dressed on site or used in unworked rubble form. MASONRY.

Strapwork

Form of decoration consisting of interlacing bands resembling straps, fretwork and art leather. It originated in the 16th C.

Stretcher

BRICKWORK

Stucco

Mixture of lime, marble dust and glue, easily fashioned but quick to set. Used for moulding figures and wall decoration. Imitation marble executed in stucco was a feature of the Baroque.

Stylobate

In Classical architecture, the base or platform on which a COLONNADE stands.

stave church of Hahnenklee

stele

strapwork

Symbols, Christian

Principal symbols found on church CAPITALS and PORTALS are:

1. Agnus Dei (Lamb of God) symbolising the sacrificial death of Christ;
2. Asp (usually a snake beneath the feet of Christ) symbolising sin (from Psalm 90 : 13);
3. A Ω (Alpha and Omega), initial and final letters of the Greek alphabet, representing the everlasting nature of God;
4. Monogram of Christ (CHR) CROSS;
5. Triangle, enclosing an eye, indicating the Trinity;
6. Unicorn, for the chastity and virginity of Mary;
7. Fish, symbol for Christ;
8. Cross, symbolising Christ's sacrifice;
9. Cross, Anchor, Heart, symbols of Faith, Hope and Charity;
10. Pelican, which, according to the legend, nourished its young on the blood from its own breast, symbolises sacrificial love;
11. Peacock, whose flesh was, according to legend, incorruptible; for the resurrection of the body;
12. Phoenix, the mythical bird which was burnt and arose out of its own ashes, symbol of the death and resurrection of Christ;
13. Signs of the Zodiac, creatures representing various months of the year; combined with a figure depicting the agricultural activity of the appropriate month.

147

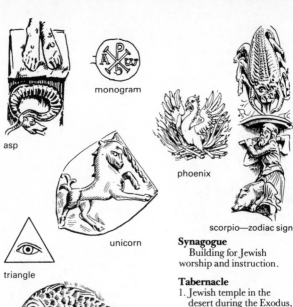

asp

monogram

phoenix

scorpio—zodiac sign

unicorn

triangle

fish

cross, anchor, heart

pelican · peacock

Synagogue
Building for Jewish worship and instruction.

Tabernacle
1. Jewish temple in the desert during the Exodus, hence any temporary place of worship;
2. Receptacle, on or above the ALTAR which contains the Holy Sacrament;
3. Free-standing canopy.

Term
HERM

Terrace
Raised level space or promenade, its limits generally defined by a balustrade. Also a row of houses of similar character.

Theatre
Greek theatres were clearly divided into three parts; the semicircular auditorium, with rising tiers of seats generally disposed on a hillside; the circular, later semicircular, orchestra which served in tragedies to accommodate dancers and chorus and in the centre of

which stood the altar of Dionysos; the stage.

The Roman theatres somewhat resembled the Greek , with a semicircular orchestra, and seats generally supported on an elaborate framework of arcades rather than following the natural slope of the ground.

Thermae

Roman baths, often on an imposing scale, centrally heated by HYPOCAUST, by means of cavity walls or hollowed floor bricks. The most important rooms were:
1. apodyterium—disrobing room;
2. frigidarium—cooling room;
3. tepidarium—warm room;
4. calidarium—hot room;
5. sudatorium—sweating chamber.

Tierceron

Intermediate RIB in Gothic VAULTING, inserted between the transverse and diagonal ribs to give additional support.

Tiled Stove

Late Gothic tiled stoves of Central Europe already had the basic shape, in the form of a cube, which has remained current. This was a square base with feet, supporting a narrower upper section which was often crowned with decorative figures. During the Renaissance, tiled stoves were more richly embellished and coloured, and, in the 16th C, often made of maiolica. Delft tiles became fashionable in the 17th C.

tabernacle set in wall

theatre

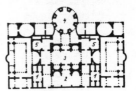

thermae

tiled stove

149

Timber-Framing

Form of construction in which walls are built as a timber framework and filled with plaster, brick, rubble, wattle and daub, etc. Also called half-timbering.

Tombs and Sepulchral Monuments

The principal forms are:
1. Memorial slab in the floor; made of stone or brass;
2. Tomb: oblong monument over a grave, sometimes with an effigy and a canopy or BALDACCHINO;
3. Sarcophagus; usually a decorated coffin made from stone, clay, wood or metal, shaped like a house, trough or chest, often bearing the recumbent effigy of the dead person;
4. Epitaph.

Torus

Convex MOULDING used at the base of columns.

Tower

From the earliest times, constructed as landmarks or lookout posts in defensive buildings. While, in the East, bells were often hung in an independent frame, in Italy the bell-tower became an adjunct to the Christian church (CAMPANILE). The elaborate use of towers in the churches and public buildings of the Middle Ages is a development both of the campanile and of the towers which flanked and sometimes surmounted city gates.

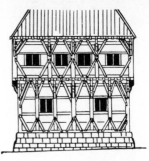

timber framing

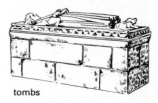

tombs

Trabeated Architecture

Greek method of building with post-and-beam, as opposed to the Roman arcuated style of building (with arches).

Tracery

Intersecting ribwork formed by the elaboration of the MULLION in the upper part of a Gothic window. Also the interlacing stone or woodwork in the VAULTING and on walls.

Trachelion

Neck of a (Greek) Doric column.

Transept

North or south transverse arm of a cruciform church.

Transom

Horizontal member dividing a window or panel.

Transverse Rib

VAULTING.

tracery

tower of town hall

gate tower

Travee
VAULTING.

Trefoil
ORNAMENT.

Triapsal or Triapsidal Plan
  Having three apses; a form characteristic of Romanesque church architecture in Central Europe.

Tribune
1. APSE of a BASILICA or basilican church;
2. Rostrum or bishop's throne;
3. Internal GALLERY of a church. It may serve to increase the floor space; to separate certain groups from the congregation at large, e. g. women, courtiers, nuns in a convent or choristers; to accommodate the organ loft; or conspicuously to divide a church. In Romanesque architecture, such galleries became a third rhythmic element between the arcading of the ground floor and the CLERESTORY. In the galleried churches of the Renaissance and Baroque, they often reached up into the vaulting itself, achieving thereby a greater sense of space.

Triforium
  Blind storey. An arcaded wall passage, open to the NAVE and situated within the wall above the nave arches, i. e., above the AISLES and below the CLERESTORY windows. A blind triforium consists of blind arcading. ▶

151

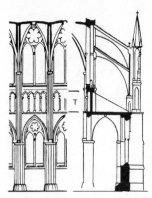

triforium (T):elevation and section

tribune

Triglyph

Block with vertical channels which distinguish the FRIEZE of a Doric ENTABLATURE.

Triptych

(Gr. triptychon—threefold structure). Tripartite picture, carving or other representation. Frequently used as a medieval winged altarpiece, with a rigid central portion and movable winged side panels.

Triumphal Arch

Form of Roman monument celebrating the triumphal procession of a victorious general through the city and, at the same time, a votive memorial. In the Renaissance the design was adapted for use on church facades.

Trophy

Various arms grouped decoratively around a breastplate, helmet or shield. Common motif, especially in 17th and 18th C, with precedents in Classical Antiquity.

triptych

trophy

Trumeau

In France, the wallspace
between two windows of the
same storey. In England a
mullion or pillar supporting
the tympanum of an arched
doorway.

Truss

Supporting framework of
a pitched ROOF.

Undercroft

Vaulted underground
room. CRYPT.

Vaulting

Arched roof, usually
composed of brick or stone,
built over an enclosed area.
In Roman and Romanesque
architecture the load of the
vaulting is carried by the
PIERS of the ARCHES and by
the solid load-bearing
masonry of the walls. In
Gothic construction it is
sustained by the piers, RIBS,
ABUTMENTS, BUTTRESSES and
flying buttresses of an
elaborate skeleton
framework, the walls
performing little or no load-
bearing function. Thus
Gothic architecture
anticipated to some extent
the conventional frame-and-
curtain-wall construction of
the 20th C.

1. Barrel or wagon vault: a
   continuous vault of semicircular or pointed
   section. It is the simplest
   form of vault. The
   masonry in-filling is
   called the web;
2. Groin vault: takes its
   name from the arched
   diagonals or groins
   formed by the intersection
   at right-angles of two
   barrel vaults. The piers
   absorb the compressive
   forces, and the
   abutments or, where
   present, flying buttresses
   resist the lateral thrust;
3. Rib vault: ribs span the
   vault in place of groins;
   they differ in section
   according to the styles of
   various periods. These
   ribs bear the load and
   guide it on to the piers.
   The web consists usually
   of light masonry. If the
   wall ribs, in order to
   increase light from a
   CLERESTORY window, are
   sprung from a higher level
   than the diagonal ribs, a
   warped web is created,
   resembling a
   ploughshare, and is then
   called a ploughshare or
   stilted vault. Long vaults
   are often broken up into
   separate bays by
   transverse ribs running at
   right-angles to a wall and
   both supporting the vault
   and defining the bay. A
   ridge rib runs along the
   longitudinal or transverse
   ridge of a vault, i. e.
   roughly 45° to the
   diagonal ribs. Rib vaults
   may be quadripartite, i. e.
   divided by two diagonal
   ribs into four compartments, or
   sexpartite, where each
   bay is divided by two
   diagonal and one
   transverse rib into six
   parts. TIERCERONS
   stemming from main
   springers between

transverse and diagonal ribs, give additional support, while LIERNES are only decorative link ribs;

4. Stellar vaults: preserving the unit of the bay, star-shaped patterns are formed by the arrangement of ribs, ridge rib, tiercerons and liernes. Net vaulting arose by abandoning the unity of each separate bay and allowing a more intricate combination of ribs which were of increasing importance. Late Gothic cellular vaults are a particular form of net vaulting found in North German brick Gothic churches. They form notch-shaped patterns;

5. Fan vaulting: ribs spread out, fan-shaped, from one point. A beautiful idiosyncrasy of the English PERPENDICULAR STYLE. Pendants hang from the centre of the intricate patterns as in the Henry VII Chapel, Westminster Abbey;

6. Domical vault: (sometimes called cloister vault) groins are semicircular instead of semi-elliptical, as in a simple groined vault. The centre of the vaulted bay, therefore, rises higher than its outer arches, like a dome. The CUPOLA is a special form of vault.

barrel vault

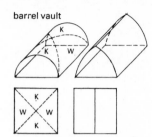

K. cross vaulting
W. Romanesque intersecting

2
crossed groin vault   K. cap vaults

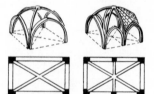

3. crossed ribbed vaulting

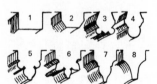

vaulting ribs in cross section:
rib profiles 1, 2. band moulding, Romanesque 11th/12th century
3, 4. circular moulding, Romanesque 12th century
5, 6, 7. pyriform moulding, Gothic 12th/14th century
8. valley moulding, late Gothic 15th century

4. stellar vaulting

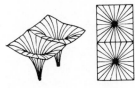

5 a. fan vaulting

5 b. fan vaulting

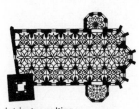

intricate vaulting

6. w. hip vaults

Vesica Piscis or **Piscium**
ORNAMENT.

Vestry
SACRISTY.

Vitruvian Scroll
   Classical undulating
spiral motif.

Volute
   Spiral scroll associated
with the Ionic CAPITAL. In a
modified form it may occur
in CONSOLES.

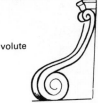

volute

Voussoirs
   Wedge-shaped stone or
brick forming an ARCH.

Wainscot, Wainscoting
   Wood panelling.

Wedge
ORNAMENT.

Westwork
   Emphatically developed
west end of a Carolingean or
Romanesque church
consisting of a low entrance
hall and, above it, a room
open to the NAVE, which is
associated with royal and
imperial functions. The
whole was crowned by one
broad tower with,
occasionally, stair turrets in
addition.

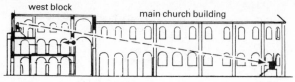

west block   main church building

westwork

westwork—interior view

winding stair turret with
spiral staircase

Winding Staircase

Spiral stairs around a central NEWEL, common in late Gothic and Renaissance architecture.

Window

Principal Elements:

1. Reveal: the internal side-surface exposed when the window is cut into the wall at right-angles;
2. Splay: the internal side surface formed when the wall is cut away obliquely;
3. Sill or Cill: the horizontal base of a window-frame;
4. LINTEL: the horizontal member spanning a window-opening, often decorated. Sometimes synonymous with ARCHITRAVE;
5. Transom; a horizontal member separating one part of a window from another;
6. Mullion: a vertical member separating one part of a window from another:
7. TRACERY: ornamental patterns formed by the branching of mullions in Gothic windows.

Some window types:

a. Round-headed: (early Christian) cut vertically into the wall. (Romanesque) splayed reveals and sill;
b. Coupled: divided by a central column into two openings or by two columns into three. Often combined as a single feature beneath blind arch. Romanesque, Renaissance;

c. Circular: (Romanesque) in Gothic generally with tracery. The round or oval Oeil-de-boeuf is typical of the Renaissance and Baroque. Oculus is a term used for any small round window;

d. Wheel windows: with radiating 'spokes';

e. Rose window: large round window with elaborate rose-like tracery, the glory of west fronts and transepts of great Gothic churches;

f. Lancet windows: tall, narrow and pointed; typical of Early English Gothic. Often grouped;

g. Pedimented: surmounted by a low-pitched gable. The pediments of such windows can be broken (the top of the triangle missing); with the vertex recessed; open (the top of the triangle open); segmental; open segmental; scrolled (with the two ends scrolled inwards); or have other variations;

h. Casement: a window with the frame hinged from the side;

i. Sash: a window, normally with the frames one above the other, with the frames or sashes sliding up and down in parallel grooves. This type was introduced in the late 17th C and became general in Britain in the 18th C. It has never been commonly used on the European continent;

j. French: a window opening to floor level in two leaves, like a pair of doors. It was probably introduced to France in the Place des Vosges, Paris (1606–12) and has remained characteristic of French domestic building and almost unmodified for nearly four centuries;

k. Venetian: a tripartite window, the middle opening arched and wider than those on either side. A favourite Palladian feature.

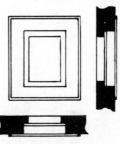

window showing reveal

window showing splay, jambs and sill

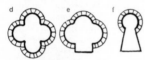

circular windows with tracery
a. four-leaved tracery (quatrefoil)
b. five-leaved tracery (cinquefoil)
c. flamboyant tracery in three parts:
   late Gothic— circular windows
   without tracery

traceried window

d. four-lobe window
e. trefoil window
f. keyhole window: Gothic

circular window

coupled window

wheel window

rose window

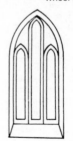

lancet window

158

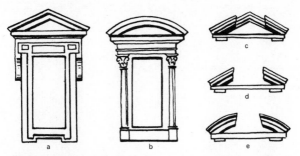

pediment and segmental arch windows
a. with simple triangular pediment
b. with segmental arch

c. chamfered pediment
d. broken pediment
e. broken segmental arch

bull's eye window

bay windows

oriel window

Wing
Building projection from the main block, rising to roof height and which may project from either the centre or ends of a building.

W   F   W

wing and frontispiece